Starting Wher

C000218264

The Story of

a Neighbourhood Centre

Liberation Theology in Practice

Kathy Galloway

First published 1998

ISBN 1-901557-04-9

We gratefully acknowledge the contribution of
THE DRUMMOND TRUST
3 PITT TERRACE, STIRLING
towards the publication costs of this book

Cover: Street Party © 1998, David Galloway
Cover photo: Lizzie McKie

Published by Wild Goose Publications, The Iona Community

The Wild Goose is a symbol of the Holy Spirit
and is the trademark of Wild Goose Publications.

Wild Goose Publications, The Iona Community,
Unit 15, Six Harmony Row, Glasgow G51 3BA

Wild Goose Publications is the publishing division of the Iona Community.
Scottish Charity No. SC003794. Limited Company Reg. No. SCO96243.

Distributed in Australia and New Zealand by Willow Connection Pty Ltd,
Unit 7A, 3-9 Kenneth Road, Manly Vale NSW 2093.

Permission to reproduce any part of this work in Australia or New Zealand
should be sought from Willow Connection.

A catalogue record for this book is available from the British Library.

Printed by The Cromwell Press Ltd, Trowbridge, Wilts.

This book is for the members of the Urban Theology Group of Orbiston and St Andrew's Churches, and for the members of these churches, and in memory of John Bowman.

I am grateful to Orbiston and St Andrew's Urban Theology Group for keeping such good records, and giving me access to them, and to George Barbour, for his help with historical material.

Martin Johnstone's writings and reflections on the process of the Urban Theology Group have been the outline which I have simply filled in. I thank him for allowing me to use them.

I wish to thank all the volunteers, staff and Board members, users of the Centre and members of the local churches and community for taking the time to talk to me and share their stories.

Kathy Galloway, March 1998

Kathy Galloway is a theologian, writer and editor. She has written *Imagining The Gospels, Love Burning Deep, Struggles to Love, Getting Personal, Talking To The Bones,* and edited the first *Iona Community Worship Book, Pushing the Boat Out, The Pattern Of Our Days* and *Dreaming of Eden.* She works in community development, lives in Glasgow and is editor of the Iona Community magazine, *Coracle.* She is a Member of the Iona Community.

An old man is scarcely, if ever, out of his house. For much of the time he just sits and grumps at the world outside. He is especially grumpy when it comes to those young lads who kick the ball into his garden, or bang on his door and then run away. This same old man played 'chap door, run' when he was young, but, according to him, 'That was just for fun. People are different nowadays.'

A young single parent got kicked out of the house when she became pregnant. Since then, her parents have had nothing to do with her. Such an attitude has coloured her impression of those who are a generation older than her. 'They just couldn't care. I made one mistake, and I enjoyed making it, and they're just going to make me pay for it for the rest of my life.'

A woman in her mid-thirties looks as if she's in her late forties. She has a severely handicapped son, and the strain of bringing him up in a place that offers him sympathy but walks the other way has cost her dear.

A man just wishes that someone would be honest enough to tell him that he will never work again, and allow him to do something creative with his life.

A wee woman says that her neighbours are good people, despite the fact that 'they're Catholics, you know.' But she cannot recognize that her neighbours are the norm rather than the exception. She has been conditioned all her life to believe that Catholics are bad, just as others have been conditioned to believe that all Protestants are evil, with the possible exception of your neighbour.

Who is my neighbour?

Introduction

*'But the teacher of the Law wanted to
justify himself, so he asked Jesus,
"Who is my neighbour?"'*

There are few stories in the New Testament which are better
known and more often quoted than that of the Good Samaritan
— and few which are harder to really put into practice.
Spontaneous response to need, unconditional kindness which
does not make value judgements about who is deserving and
who is not, practical support of the kind that is appropriate
and often costly — these are more demanding than we usually
admit when we preach this text.

Because it is difficult to put into practice, it is, therefore, all
the more remarkable how often it actually happens, how often
people ask the question, 'who is my neighbour?', hear the
answer, 'anyone who is in need', and seek to discover and
practise what it means to be kind. Such kindness may be taken
for granted, undervalued, or even go unnoticed. Perhaps that
says something about the people our society also takes for
granted, undervalues, or even fails to notice. A member of
royalty is feted for visiting strangers in hospital, a famous
sportsman praised for his support of a charity — and all power
to them — and yet tens of thousands of ordinary people do
these things and more every day, with no thought of personal
profit, no motive apart from kindness, no reason other than
that they care.

This is the story of such a group of ordinary people. Because
they care, they are like millions of others. All over the world,
people care about friends and loved ones, about strangers, even
about enemies. Like the people in this story, many of them care

in the midst of difficult, even dreadful situations and circumstances, and some of them in the horrors of war, famine and extreme degradation. They too have their stories. But each story has its specifics, its own distinguishing features, its characters, the things that make it unique. A story which has much in common with human stories from every time and place also has its own concrete time and place. It has a *here* and it has a *now*. And it has a *who*.

So here are some of the specifics of this story. Its *here* is a housing scheme called Orbiston in a town called Bellshill in North Lanarkshire, west central Scotland. Its *now* are the years from 1991-1996. Its *who* are the people of that community, and in particular, the people who make up the Orbiston Neighbourhood Centre — those who dreamed it and made the dream a reality, those who use it, those who work in it and those who support it.

These people, in this place and this time, asked questions about how best to care, how best to love their neighbours. There are particular aspects of this process of asking questions and discovering, if not answers, then directions to go in, which are worth sharing — if only because people have wanted to know about them. The *'how' of* care is always important, because it is in the 'how' that theory becomes practice, intentions become actions, that we practise what we preach. 'How' is where the word becomes flesh.

So this is a story about *how* this group of people made their care active. There are a number of points to emphasize here, which will come up again in the story.

A Local Church Story

First, this is the story of two local churches, Orbiston and St Andrew's, Bellshill. A local or parish church, that is, one whose members are drawn from, and which seeks to serve the area in which its buildings are situated, is an interesting thing from the point of view of its size, because it operates at a kind of intermediate level between the individual and the institutional. Within a local church, people act in a way that is not just the response or initiative of one person, but collective action. But collectively, they still have the freedom to act directly. They can set priorities, decide strategies, make choices, with relatively little external pressure or interference. Within the constraints of their own particular context, (be these of money, personnel, vision or values) they have quite a high degree of autonomy. Decisions can be (in fact, must *be*) made at the grassroots, and the people who make the decisions are the same people who take the action. They also, of course, have to assume the responsibility for the success or failure of the action, and bear any consequences that arise from it. They stand or fall by their own commitment.

Most of the collective action in our society has severed the link between decision and action. Education, health, social services, housing, economic policy are all decided upon on our behalf, by people we have elected to do that job for us. Apart from casting our vote every five years or so, most of us have little or no influence at all on the decisions that are then made about these things. We may be involved in the action that is then taken to implement these decisions through our work, as employees of the National Health Service, in education as anything from headteachers to school cleaners, as home helps or social workers, and so on. We will certainly be affected by it, as pupils or parents, as patients, as workers, as taxpayers or as benefit claimants.

But if we don't like the action taken on our behalf, if we feel it affects us, or our society, adversely, then we are limited in what we can do. Local government is progressively weakened, and has its powers taken away from it to be handed to non-elected and non-accountable quangos, trusts, or in Scotland, taken directly into the remit of the Secretary of State. Trade unions too have been weakened by legislation, their numbers falling, and business and industry generally becomes evermore distant and accountable only to boards and shareholders in faraway places. Some who have the time and energy and inclination may campaign or lobby on single issues. But they too are unable to mend the link between decision and action.

Because in so many areas of our lives we feel passive, acted-upon rather than actors, with little sense that we can affect or change the decisions that purport to be made on our behalf, it is very easy for people to feel powerless. Powerlessness is a dangerous feeling. It can make us feel angry and frustrated, with a tendency to lash out at those we *can* reach — our families, our neighbours, our own immediate environment. It can make us inflict hurt or damage on ourselves. Or it can make us more and more depressed, apathetic and hopeless, until we give up caring about anything.

Therefore, any group or organization that operates at this intermediate level, that reconnects decisions and actions, is important, because it has the possibility of giving people back some power in their lives. To be part of a group is to immediately enlarge the scope of action we can take — and many of our problems are simply beyond the strength or resources of the individual. And to be part of a group which still has the power to act on its decisions, which is mutually accountable, is the beginning of a way out of a cycle of apathy and hopelessness.

There are many local community groups of this kind in

Scotland, from tenants associations to credit unions, from Women's Aid to community arts organizations. Local churches are among the longest-established of such groups. As such, they have a number of distinctive features. They usually have deep roots in their area, hundreds of years in older areas, and since their beginnings in the case of housing schemes. They have a name, an identity and an easily recognizable building. Their building, although it may have its own problems of upkeep, appropriateness and scale, may nevertheless be one of the few, or indeed the only public building in the area with the size and flexibility for communal activities.

And they have existing structures for organizing. There isn't a church in the country which doesn't have decades of experience of running meetings, whether church managers, boards and committees, or in outward-looking youth clubs, parents and toddlers groups or a whole host of other activities. There is a wealth of experience of social structures (including the corresponding fundraising) in any local church. They're used to making things happen.

And a local church has a well-developed symbolic framework which is part of its ongoing life. Week by week, its members meet, remind themselves of who they are, take an audit of their personal and corporate failures and achievements, their strengths and weaknesses, assume responsibility for their failures (in the language of the church, this is called confession) and are released from being defined by these. They give thanks for what they perceive to be loving and hopeful in their lives, and intentionally call to mind the needs and suffering of others. They commit themselves once again to each other, and to working in caring ways for the realization of their vision. Local churches, therefore, have practical and historical and symbolic resources available to them that many secular organizations would give their eye teeth for.

Of course, the idea of the Christian vision may strike horror into the hearts of many, especially for those whose experience of the church, in childhood or adulthood, has been of authoritarian and narrow-minded institutions, purveying bigotry, moralizing and cultural imperialism, and controlling and manipulating vulnerable people through a mixture of fear and hypocrisy. And indeed, it would be wrong to suggest that elements of all these things do not still exist — as they do in all institutions that are made up of fallible human beings who engage with issues of power and powerlessness.

But just as society has changed, so has the church, and a visitor to most local churches would find a group of people simply struggling to articulate a vision of what it means to love the neighbour who we can see out of a love for the God we cannot see, in very practical ways. One of the very real benefits of living in a pluralist society in which the claims of social or religious conformity have been weakened is that churches are now much more likely to be constituted by those who are there by conviction, not just because it is expected of them.

And especially in poor areas, local churches often display genuine sacrificial love, bereft of pietism, because there is no chance of mistaking the grace of God for worldly prosperity. The vision is likely to be more inclusive, more ecumenical, more self-critical and more down-to-earth than in the past. And just as the church institutionally is now as likely to find itself lambasted by politicians and the media alike for drawing attention to the limitations of free-market economic theories, or for its critique of our country's military adventures as for being 'the Tory Party at prayer', so it is the case that many local community activists are as likely to come from the local churches as from the local branches of political parties — and are actually often in both groups!

A Care in the Community Story

This is also the story of how this local church engaged with a major piece of social legislation. Care in the Community is the name given to the policy in recent years of keeping those people in our society who are vulnerable, who require to be cared for because they are unable to do it themselves, in the communities to which they belong — and in many instances, of closing down the large, centralized institutions in which they had been previously cared for and releasing them back into the community. Though there is widespread agreement that the principle of Care in the Community is fine, allowing people to maintain family links, to live more normal lives and to maintain the highest degree of independent living possible, practice has been a somewhat different matter. With the responsibility for care being put back on families, there is also widespread agreement that such families have been under-resourced, under-supported, and all too often, just left to sink or swim.

And where people have no families, or cannot live with their families for a range of reasons, Care in the Community has been expected to be provided either by a voluntary sector which is overstretched, under-resourced and had insufficient time to prepare for the new responsibilities placed on it, or has been privatized into the hands of private companies whose bottom line is all too often their profit margin and their shareholders. Care becomes a commodity, and the goodwill of many working in this sector has not prevented some tragic instances of abuse.

There are some people who even fall through these fragile safety nets. We have become familiar in recent years with the plight of young people, many of whom have come out of social service residential care at the age of sixteen with no family backup, and without the personal resources to cope with independent living. The withdrawal of state benefit for sixteen- to eighteen-year-olds has sharpened this hard edge, and for many of them, care in the community has in practice meant homelessness, unemployment, and the drift into drug addiction and prostitution.

Equally familiar has become the sight of people with mental health problems, some of them having spent years in institutions which had become their homes, losing even this level of stability when their homes were shut down. Distressed, isolated, they have been further isolated by the fact that their distress can assume a frightening face to people unfamiliar with their situation. The community has been ill-equipped to support such vulnerable people.

And yet, even in such adverse circumstances, a vast amount of good practice in care continues. People and organizations have found creative ways of using and interpreting the Care in the Community legislation. This is one such story.

A Liberation Theology Story

One of the quite unusual features of this story is that it introduces an idea that is more familiar to us (if indeed, it's familiar at all) from other parts of the world, particularly from the Third World. Liberation theology is a term first used by the Brazilian theologian Gustavo Gutierrez which reads the Bible from the perspective/through the eyes of poor and dispossessed people, encourages them to see themselves as the subjects of their own life rather than as the object of other people's understanding of them (whether that understanding be one of pity or of contempt) is inspired by the great narratives of the Bible, particularly the story of the Exodus (the liberation of the Jewish people from oppression in Egypt, hence the term 'liberation') by the prophetic calls for justice of the Old Testament, and by Jesus' proclamation of the kingdom. It has struck deep chords in places where structures of injustice and economic dependence oppress great numbers of people (as the Gospel indeed did among the poor and oppressed of Jesus' own time, and in many eras since. From it is derived the notion of the 'bias to/preferential option for the poor.'

Though Latin-American liberation theology is still the best-known form, other liberation theologies have also been developed, whose common feature is that they read the Scriptures from the perspective of different groups which have in different ways experienced exclusion or oppression. So there is black liberation theology (both African and American), Asian liberation theology (*minjung*), a wide range of women's liberation theologies and gay liberation theology, and the liberation theologies of indigenous peoples. These have often gone hand in hand with an attempt to reconstruct or rediscover the hidden histories of these groups — their stories of hope and struggle, their saints and martyrs, whose details have been concealed because they did not serve the interests of those in power.

As much as a theory, liberation theology is a methodology, a way of doing things, a process. It enquires about justice, does its theology not in a university or church context, but out of the experience of engagement in the public arena, whether that be the street or the factory, the marketplace or the parliament. Its basic model is that of *praxis,* meaning 'to do.' That is, its reflection, study and prayer arises out of its practical engagement, its doing, and not out of theorizing. This reflection in turn sets the context for further action, and so on, in an ongoing process of action/reflection/action. The truth of an idea or belief is not based on whether it is intellectually justifiable or doctrinally pure, but by whether it brings about transformation in the lives of persons and communities, and in the structures that shape their lives.

Orbiston is, in Scottish terms, a poor area. Both Orbiston and St Andrew's Churches made a conscious decision to follow the methodology of liberation theology in their attempt to discover what it meant to love their neighbours. Again, it is important to stress that this was not some obscure theory. For them, it was a way of reading the Bible, of praying, of sharing deeply and self-critically in reflection on their own very practical, indeed, often mundane action. It is not a political agenda or blueprint — but it proved to have political and economic implications.

A Story of People

All the best stories are about people. Partly that's because we need people in a story to draw us in, to identify with, to care about what happens to them in the course of the action, and real people have the most riveting stories. There's something compelling about knowing that 'this really happened. It's not just fiction.' And stories about real people therefore include not just their achievements but their failures, not just their hopes but their sorrows, not just their strengths but their weaknesses, because that's what real life is like.

And partly it's because, in the end, nothing happens without people. They're the actors, they drive the action, moved by their concerns and their loves, their fears and their care. No theory can ever act as an agent for change without the people who make it happen, who, day by day, show up and do all the small tasks, attend to the innumerable details of making things happen. So this story is above all about people, not people in the abstract, but real, specific individuals with names. It's about

John and Nancy, Martin and Evelyn, Anita and Annabelle, John and Shirley and Susan, Irene and John and Marion and May and Duncan and a whole host of others, about their faith and commitment and care. It's about being a neighbour.

1
This Time, This Place

Reading the History in the Geography

The first thing a storyteller has to do is to start. That's sometimes more difficult than it seems. Where to start? When did it all begin, and how? So perhaps a good place to start is with the place itself, by telling something of its *geography*, where it is on the map and what it looks like. And since any place is affected and shaped and changed by what people do in it and with it, that means telling something of its *history* too.

Bellshill is a small town of about twenty thousand people in North Lanarkshire in the Central Belt of the lowlands of Scotland. It lies ten miles east of Glasgow and thirty-five miles west of Edinburgh, and a couple of miles south of the M8, the motorway which connects Scotland's two main cities. A local railway line runs through the town. The county of Lanark itself is divided into two easily distinguished parts. South Lanarkshire is rural, sparsely populated, and beautiful, a landscape of rolling hills, rivers running through green valleys, small villages and market towns. It is an agricultural area, dairy and arable farming, and the Clydesdale valley is famous for the berries which grow so well in its mild, damp climate.

North Lanarkshire, on the other hand, is urban, densely populated and less obviously beautiful to the passing observer, marked as it is by the remains of its industrial past. For here, we are in the heartland of industrial Scotland — except that now it would more properly be described as post-industrial. Once upon a time, this too was agricultural land, and, one imagines, much like its southern half. But it has had a different history. In many ways, it is possible to read the social and economic history of Scotland from the small town of Bellshill alone. As late as the eighteenth century, this was still farming land, and the only industry to speak of was that of the weavers, carrying on their production from cottage looms. Its population was then only a few hundred.

A Microcosm of Change

But the nineteenth century brought with it the greatest change this place had seen in millennia. The Industrial Revolution transformed the face of the Central Belt of Scotland. A few miles away, the city of Glasgow, with its great port at the mouth of the Clyde, became the 'second city of the British Empire'. On the banks of the Clyde, from Glasgow all the way to Greenock, shipyards began building the ships that sailed the world, and brought the raw materials — the cotton, the jute, the rubber and much more — back to be processed in the factories and mills of the Central Belt. Hundreds of them sprang up in Lanarkshire, with its easy access to the river Clyde and its port, and thence to the sea.

Easy access too, to labour. The farmworkers and weavers found themselves with a very different way of life, not now living off the land, or from the products of family, cottage industry, but instead, working long hours for wages. The numbers of the native people were swelled by the Highlanders and islanders forced off their land by that tragic and shameful episode in Scottish history, the Highland Clearances.

Already suffering for their support of the defeated Jacobite cause in the Risings of 1715 and 1745, culminating in the slaughter of the Battle of Culloden; their ancient clan system

23

severely weakened by the punitive measures meted out against them in the aftermath of the '45, the people of the Highlands were dealt a death blow by their own clan chiefs. Having tasted a more expensive 'good life' (often when in exile in other parts of Europe), and with the move away from a feudal, subsistence economy to a capitalist economy, it became clear to these landowners that Highland land could be more profitably utilized as sporting estates, and, more particularly, in raising sheep, than in supporting a considerable population of small farmers. The population had to be reduced, and, with great severity and a number of considerable atrocities (to which the church, in some cases, turned a blind eye, or even gave its blessing to) men and women and children were driven off the land.

But they had to go somewhere. Some of them were driven down to the coastal areas, eking out a hard living fishing and beachcombing. Tens of thousands of them shipped on board vessels bound for the other side of the world, in an exodus that drained the Highlands of whole generations of young people; to Australia, to the United States, and most of all, to the Dominion of Canada. And tens of thousands more, needing to live and feed their children, made their way to the source of jobs, to the industrial heartland of Scotland, including North Lanark. They brought with them a Gaelic language, culture and way of life very different to that of the Lowlands, to become part of the huge population explosion of nineteenth-century Lanark. Many parts of that culture survive to this day, and the Highland names still take up pages in the telephone book.

Fuel for the Engine

An economic transformation like the one that took place in nineteenth-century Britain had to be powered. The ships, the factories, the mills, the yards, the ironworks, and the homes of their millions of workers needed to be fuelled by something. Lanarkshire, like many other parts of Scotland, became a coal-mining county. For more than a hundred years, the industry that provided the wealth and military power that gave Britain an Empire was driven by coal dug by, among others, Lanarkshire miners. But the miners who went under the ground, working long hours in dangerous and difficult conditions, often dying young from respiratory diseases, did not become rich. Coalfields all over Scotland, England and Wales threw their characteristic workings, their pit machinery, their slag heaps and bings, their colliery rows and mining villages on to previously rural landscapes. Perhaps no industry has ever marked its territory so clearly. But it was a landscape which bore the marks of poverty. Bellshill became a mining town, and its population grew.

At the dawn of the twentieth century, Scotland, as part of this great industrial empire, saw its future as leading ever onwards to greater prosperity and progress. Even the First World War, with its huge loss of life, did not halt the momentum. A war needs ships, munitions — and coal. But the end of the war brought a new mood of fear and uncertainty. No longer a war economy, economic downturn on a worldwide scale was beginning to threaten. Fewer ships were being built. Jobs became scarcer and more insecure. In America, the stock market crashed, ruining tens of thousands, and the tremors were felt across the globe. Britain too entered the Depression.

In this economic climate, people felt once again the chill wind of poverty and fear. It is not perhaps surprising, therefore, that the latest wave of immigration into North Lanarkshire, was greeted with such hostility. Since the famines of the nineteenth century, the poor people of Ireland too had been emigrating in search of survival in the first place, and a better life beyond.

Some of them came to Scotland, many to work as labourers in the great building projects of the early part of this century, and in turn, more and more came to join them.

To people worried about their jobs, there was clearly a perceived sense of threat from this influx (though not much evidence to support it). But much more than this was the fact that this group of people, in many ways resembling the Highland migrants of the nineteenth century with their roots in Gaeldom, was, in other important respects quite different.

From the Other Side of the Sea

The Scottish Gaels, for all their different language, shared the same religious adherence. The majority of them were Protestants, Presbyterian like the local population (though often belonging to stricter persuasions of these). The newcomers, on the other hand, were Roman Catholic, at a time when it was not good to be either Irish or Catholic in Britain. The movement for Irish emancipation, and all the turbulence arising from, and following that, the Easter Rising, the activities of the Black and Tans in Ireland, the founding of the Irish Free State and the partition of Ireland had caused further deep wounds in the already wounded relationship between the countries on either side of the Irish Sea. The suspicion of Irish people (perhaps heightened by the guilt of those who recognized the injustices perpetrated on Ireland by a colonial Britain) was at its height.

And for many (perhaps most) Protestants, brought up to believe at best in Roman Catholicism as the main threat to their religious and political freedoms, and at worst as an apostate heresy, worshipping the Antichrist in Rome, it must have been easy to project other fears on to the followers of what seemed an alien faith, and therefore to believe their culture, language and way of life to be inferior. The Church in Scotland, which might have helped in many ways to allow fearful people to become more tolerant and accepting of what were, in fact, poor and struggling communities with less religious and political rights than Protestants, failed in this task. To its eternal disgrace, there are records of the Church of Scotland in the 1920s which show that its highest courts fed this bigotry, and called for repatriation of 'inferior peoples'.

This tension was heightened in Lanarkshire because so many Scottish Protestants there had family connections with the Ulster Loyalists, Scots who had migrated to Ulster as part of Oliver Cromwell's Plantations in the seventeenth century. Protestant, mostly Presbyterian, fiercely loyal to the British Crown, they had formed the backbone of Edward Carson's Ulster Volunteers, whose resistance to the founding of the Irish Free State had led to the partition of Ireland. Scottish Protestants in counties like Lanarkshire demonstrated their solidarity with their kinsfolk in Ulster by joining branches of loyalist organizations like the Orange Lodge.

These tensions were to spill over into sectarian division that cut through Lanarkshire like a knife, and that often erupted into violence. Over this century, it became a divided county, with 'Protestant' towns and 'Catholic' towns, 'Protestant' councils and 'Catholic' councils, 'Protestant' businesses and 'Catholic' businesses. The Catholic community was enlarged further by immigration into the area of Lithuanian refugees. The introduction of separate Catholic schools, seen by Catholics as a necessary medium for educating children with religious and communitarian values in a way which state education did not allow for, was deeply resented by Protestants, and became a symbol of alienation. The marks of this sectarianism are still visible today, in Bellshill as elsewhere in Lanarkshire.

Days of Steel

Depression, pit closure, poverty, sectarianism! It was a gloomy picture for Bellshill. And yet, with a resilience that seems to be a pattern over the centuries, Bellshill once again re-invented itself, this time as a steel town. In the economic rebuilding in the aftermath of the Second World War, and in the drive to the affluent society, a consumer boom saw, not just the wealthy, but ordinary people demand the labour-saving devices, the white goods and above all, the cars of the new society. Now what was needed was steel.

Bellshill sits in the shadow of steel strip mills, and the closest of them all is Ravenscraig — at least it was, until it was demolished in 1996. For decades, Ravenscraig and Clydesdale produced steel for British industry, until finally, after increasing productivity and efficiency constantly for years, and after a desperate fight for survival, they were closed, as part of a deliberate government strategy of running down heavy industry in the Central Belt. In this town, hundreds of people either worked at 'the 'Craig' or Clydesdale or in related, ancillary businesses. It was another body-blow to its economy. Once again, it was back to the days of redundancies, job insecurity and fear for the future.

In the few years since then, Bellshill, like much of North Lanarkshire, has been marked by high unemployment, low morale, social deprivation and the things it carries in its wake — young people with not much purpose or hope in their lives, alcohol and drug abuse, family breakdown and a general air of malaise. There have been some small signs of an upturn in the job situation; a large supermarket distribution plant, plans for a new industrial initiative, jobs in tourism and leisure. But many of these are low-paid jobs, or in fields for which the skills are too specific to make a large difference. For many, especially school leavers and those over forty, the prospects are still bleak.

It would be easy to write off Bellshill as a depressed and depressing place, with not much going for it at all. What would draw you about a place whose natural beauty has been so scarred, with no glories of architecture or town planning to redeem that, where there are few jobs and not much money, with all the problems of poverty and a sad sectarian history. You'd think people would be lining up to get away from the place. But you'd be wrong!

One of the interesting things about Lanarkshire is the strength of the links between the place and the people. A recent study showed that the county has the lowest mobility rates in the whole of Scotland (around eleven per cent). There are families that go back generations in the same place — and when people have to move (as, for example, when the inhabitants of the miners' rows just outside Bellshill in the community known locally as 'The Pailace' had to leave their homes because the whole area was being flooded to make the lake of Strathclyde Country Park) they mostly choose to move as nearby as they can.

Even presented with a better alternative, people will not necessarily take it. The story is told of a young man who left Bellshill and went away to university in England. He trained as a teacher, and returned to Scotland hoping to get a teaching job in the west of Scotland, but none was forthcoming. He knew he could get a job by going back to England, but decided he would rather remain in Scotland unemployed than leave his home town again! In this area, there is an incredible sense of belonging, of loyalty to the place.

A Sense of Community

This is a place with a strong sense of its own identity, with a rich social history and memory. In part, perhaps, that's a result of a history of shared struggle, forged in hard times over generations. And though its religious history has been so tainted with sectarianism, it's worth remembering that it has also given people a sense of value, of being worth caring about. When much of the natural and social environment has been hostile, it has been the communal bonds which have been strong enough to keep people rooted on this particular piece of Scotland, holding fast in the relationship, finding civic pride and seeking out the best in a landscape that offers no quick rewards or immediate gratification.

But whether the bonds of community can survive the individualist, 'me-first' cultural pressures of the present remains to be seen, and is a serious and worrying question. There are already signs of their weakening in the fear of many elderly people of being out at night or answering their doors, in random violence and vandalism, in the breakdown of family relationships.

Perhaps one of the resources from its history that Bellshill has to draw on is its long radical tradition. It has been used to trying new things. And it's been good at standing out against the status quo in defence of its rights. The social experiment of the radical reformer and millowner Robert Owen at nearby New Lanark is known worldwide. His model village for his mill-owners, his educational programmes for their children, his early attempts at worker participation and a form of stakeholding have found many imitators, and tens of thousands of tourists come to visit the restored village every year.

But less well known is the fact that Owen attempted an earlier version in Bellshill, in a community with the name later given to the Bellshill housing scheme, Orbiston, settled on the ancient lands where the name originated. Some of the street names in present-day Orbiston bear witness to this early experiment — Community Road, Liberty Road. This one, however, was less successful. Some of the douce townspeople took exception to what they considered to be the loose moral tone of the place, (they had dancing on a Saturday night!) felt it encouraged drunkenness, and generally gave it short shrift. It was known locally as 'Babylon' — and so today, there is also a Babylon Road!

Another, perhaps more lasting testimony to the dissenting tradition of Bellshill lies in its church history. St Andrew's Church, Bellshill, one of the two churches at the heart of this story, was founded in 1762, and was proudly known as 'the first Relief church in the West.' To make sense of this rather mysterious title, it is necessary to understand a little of the history of Scottish Presbyterianism.

The Claims of Liberty

One of the fundamental principles of the Scottish Reformation was that of religious freedom — liberty of conscience. The right to worship God in their own way, using the language, forms of worship and church government and theological insights that had arisen from their particular culture and experience motivated Scots in the sixteenth and seventeenth centuries to resist, (and at some points to join battle with) those external bodies which sought to impose other practices. The external bodies were both ecclesiastical (the Roman Catholic church, particularly as symbolized by the Papacy, and later, the Anglican Church of England) and secular (the Scottish aristocracy, the monarchy, and, in the seventeenth century, the British state itself). By the eighteenth century, these bodies no longer posed a threat to religious liberty, and certain freedoms were enshrined in law and practice. But the struggle was not yet over, and this time, the conflict was to tear apart Presbyterianism itself.

One of the practices that had come to mark the Church of Scotland was that of patronage, whereby the local landowner or laird could 'present' a parish with a new minister when the church fell vacant. This privilege (really a hangover from a time in the past when landowners could tell their tenants how to worship) meant that he could effectively choose what kind of leadership the parish had, gave him considerable power and influence as the 'patron' of the minister, and was obviously open to abuse. It was deeply resented by the people, who, perhaps being touched by the new democratic spirit of the age (this was the century of the American and French Revolutions, after all) felt they had the right to choose their own minister.

In 1762, the congregation of the Parish of Bothwell (a few miles from Bellshill) were 'presented' with a new minister by the patrons of the church. Calling as their justification the Book of Order of the Reformation, which stated 'The presentation of the people must be preferred. This liberty with all care must be reserved till [in Scots, till = to] every several kirk.', the majority of the congregation refused to accept the minister, withdrew from the building and began to worship in the open air in surrounding parts of Lanarkshire. Eventually, in 1763, they were given land in Bellshill on which to build, and so the Relief Church was born.

For almost a hundred years, it remained outside the

established Church of Scotland. It had been in the vanguard of dissent from the establishment, and drew dissenters from a wide area. It remained 'open to all those oppressed in their Christian privileges,' with an enthusiastic preaching tradition, and much practical pioneering work in worship, mission and the care of the poor. In 1847, when the whole Church of Scotland split down the middle over the issue of patronage, in the event known as The Disruption, the Relief Church joined with all the other churches which had seceded from the Church of Scotland in the United Presbyterian Church.

In 1929, after nearly a century of fragmentation in Presbyterianism was being repaired in reunion, the Relief Church came back into the Church of Scotland, and took a new name, St Andrew's 'but we have no right to this honoured name unless we are an active, progressive and missionary church.' St Andrew's remains today the 'town' church, with its building at the heart of the town at Bellshill Cross.

As the town had grown, other churches were established: Bellshill West and Macdonald Memorial Churches of Scotland, Bellshill Baptist Church, a Congregational church, the Salvation Army, and three Roman Catholic churches reflecting the changing population, Sacred Heart, St Gerard's and Holy Family. For a small town, Bellshill has many churches.

In the postwar reconstruction that led to the building of local authority housing schemes all over urban Scotland, the old name of Orbiston had been given to one such scheme on the edge of Bellshill. The Church of Scotland had sought to give each of these areas their own church in a massive scheme in the 1950s and 1960s known as Church Extension, and in 1954, Orbiston Church was founded. These were growth times for the church in Scotland — a youthful population attended in large numbers, and used the community facilities that in the earlier days of the Welfare State often only the churches could provide, especially in the schemes.

But in the changing social and religious climate of the 1970s and 1980s, numbers began to decline. Populations became more mobile, and large Victorian churches increasingly costly to maintain, were inappropriate for their purposes. A process known as Union and Readjustment began in the Church of Scotland, and shared some of the same processes as were happening in the industrial economy. Many churches were deemed redundant to requirements, the congregations were dispersed to other churches, buildings were closed down and sold off. Others were united, sometimes willingly, often not. Some were given ministers on terminable appointments (essentially a fixed-term in which to turn the decline around). And many more were linked, a process whereby each church retained its own buildings and identity, but shared many more of its institutions (and most especially, its minister). It was a thoroughgoing downsizing!

In 1980, the congregations of St Andrew's Bellshill and Orbiston were linked into one parish — the oldest church in the town, and the youngest. The one had a long and rich history, a fine building and a place in the heart of the town. The other was in the middle of a housing scheme with huge social problems. What could these two churches do together?

2
New Eyes for Reading The Bible

Finding a Different Way

When people in Orbiston and Saint Andrew's Churches are asked what the precise order of things happening was, they can't quite remember what came first. It's the old question of when was the beginning; was it when Martin Johnstone, the new minister, came in 1989 — or the 1991 summer mission — or the setting up of the urban theology group in the same year? Or was it in fact simply a new chapter of an ongoing story, which had turned over onto a clean page back in 1980, when a housing scheme church set in the midst of an area beset with poverty, unemployment and social upheaval was linked with a church with a two-hundred-year history of radical faith and practical engagement with the needs of the community?

Whatever the exact timeline was, there is general agreement about some things. In the summer of 1991, a group of young people came to do a summer mission in Orbiston. Part of that was a Scripture Union-inspired phenomenon called the 'Light Factory,' which involved covering the entire inside of Orbiston Church in cardboard and silver foil! Whatever it was meant to represent, it was obviously a great success with the local children. About 250 primary-school children took part. At the end of the mission, the team, augmented by local members, undertook a visit to the homes of every child who had participated, in an effort to encourage their families to become involved in the normal church activities. The response was disappointing; a resounding zero. No one seemed at all interested.

This led members of the linked churches, many of whom had worked very hard on the mission, to begin to ask some serious questions about the nature of their activities as the church. Why had this approach not worked? What should or could their response as Christians be to the problems they saw in their neighbourhood (problems which they themselves shared)? Was there a better way for them to use their time and energies? Kirk Session meetings were held asking questions about the use of the church buildings; could they be more appropriately used? Could they learn from the experience of other churches?

About this time, a friend of Martin's suggested that perhaps it might be an idea to enrol him to do a Master of Ministry as an external, part-time degree, at the Urban Theology Unit in Sheffield (whose university validated the unit's degrees). This might be a good vehicle for a group to get together to look at the whole idea of urban theology.

The Urban Theology Unit is an innovative centre founded by Revd Dr John Vincent, a former President of the Methodist Church in Britain, to take theology out of the academic sphere and into the places where people live and work and struggle with the questions of daily existence. From its inception, it has emphasized the public and social function of theology, and has sought to reunite the practical and experiential with the theoretical, believing that theology is done where people are, and in fact, cannot be done without addressing itself to the serious issues of poverty, unemployment and urban malaise which affect so many of Britain's cities. Staff members of the UTU have lived in community, and as part of the neighbourhoods they were considering.

In many ways, they have been an example of aspects of the liberation theology of Latin America, but in a British context.

This is true as much of its methods of working as in its content. It has taken as its raw material not the writings of academics and 'experts', but the data of people's everyday reality, considering them to be the real experts in the interpretation of their own experience. From that perspective, they have read the Bible and allowed it to speak to them and through them. It has tried to help people to be the subjects of their theologizing, and not the objects of other people's speculation. Put simply, just as Latin American *campesinos* (peasants) *could* read the stories of the Exodus, and see how their experience of oppression and injustice was reflected in the slavery of the Israelites, poor people in Britain could also read the Bible in a new way. They could be allowed, and encouraged, to identify, not with the pious and religious church people, but with the outcast and marginalized.

Theology: a community activity

The idea of enrolling in the UTU was attractive to Martin, who already had a deep interest in liberation theology. Martin had come to Orbiston and St Andrew's as his first charge. He had studied academic theology and gained his degree at Aberdeen University. But his view of theology had changed somewhat from the past. From seeing theology as a discipline in which knowledge was passed on from theology teachers to ministers, and hence to their congregations (a 'top-down' model), he had come to see it as essentially a community-based exercise in which the 'professional' brought knowledge and skills in one area (that of traditional/historical theology) while others in the community brought *their* areas of expertise (such as the traditions and culture of their church and community, and the social, economic and political conditions existing in the community).

In this view of theology, all the participants had one thing in common; 'faith in the power of God to change things, and a commitment to sharing in that change. Theology was no longer a knowledge of the mind, but also a knowledge of the heart.' It was not simply intellectual, or arguing a case. It was also liberating. It set people free.

Some of this shift came about through his own unease with the apparent disregard for the poor and the young in the institutional church. Some came from his own experience of loss and grief at the death of his father. Much came from his experience as assistant minister in Castlemilk, a large peripheral scheme in Glasgow. Of that time Martin wrote:

'... I realized, as never before, the special privilege it is to learn from those whom Jesus called blessed ...'

and again:

'... among those people I have experienced great theological truths, (such as the universal love of God for all people, God's hatred of injustice, his real sharing with the poor, and his condemnation of the idolatry of the age and of the church. These lessons forced me to recognize one other often forgotten theological truth, 'Father, Lord of heaven and earth! I thank you because you have shown to the unlearned what you have hidden from the wise and learned. Yes, father, this is how you wanted it to happen.' (Luke 10: 21)

After his time in Castlemilk, Martin had gone back to university, and had done research into the need for liberation theology in a British context. But perhaps it was most of all in Castlemilk that for Martin the truth of something Martin Luther said was clearest:

38

'A man becomes a theologian by living, by dying and by being damned, not by understanding, reading and speculating.'

This proposal went to the kirk sessions; a group would work on group-building and collective action, and the Urban Theology Unit course would act as an external reference point. The response of the two sessions was positive and enthusiastic. The go-ahead was given, and the group, and the course, were started in autumn 1991.

Initially, the UTU wanted the focus of the degree to be on Martin's own ministry, with the group as a support group. But the Bellshill folk saw what they were embarking on much more as the ministry of the whole group, and Martin as their representative in this new learning, and this was the way they proceeded. So there was a note of tension with the UTU right from the beginning. Nevertheless, with a sense of excitement, the group embarked on this three-year programme, which involved Martin in two days every two months in Sheffield. The Session also were to be constantly updated on progress. This was a group working on behalf of a much larger body.

There were about a dozen of them, and that number remained fairly constant, though of course, not everyone could make every meeting. It would be a mistake to think that they set out with a clear vision or agenda for what they were doing. They were tentative, unsure of their suitability for the task facing them, unsure about whether they were going in the right direction. Early meetings were characterized by confusion, and the struggle to discern some outlines or signposts to follow. Nevertheless, there was an exciting dimension to the work during these early months, and an almost Abrahamic sense of setting out on a journey. Looking back, the group would say that although they didn't always know what was happening (and still, often, don't) they believe that God did (and does).

Commitment, faith and experience: the starting point of theology

When you're not quite sure where you're going, or even how you're going to get there, perhaps there will be clues in the ground you're presently standing on. And this is what the Urban Theology Group (its new name) did. They didn't begin by drawing up plans of action. They didn't even begin with the Bible. They began by simply telling their own stories. This group of ordinary people shared their experience, not as experts coming in from outside, or as a nice cosy church group unaffected by the things going on around them, but simply as people who shared a common faith, and a commitment to trying to change the malaise they saw around them.

Some of these stories were joyful ones. One of the members of the group was a man called John Bowman, who had fought alcoholism for many years. After eventually getting sober, he had become deeply involved in church and community affairs, (he had long been involved in politics!) was an elder and a local councillor. His story was one of gratitude for a dozen years of sobriety. He was to play a crucial role in the group as an encourager; his sense of humour, of hope and of determination often kept others going when the obstacles seemed too great to overcome.

Other were tales of continued hardship; of bringing up a disabled son with limited community facilities. This was a group of people who had experience of the problems they were seeking to address. They knew within their number the pain of unemployment, of disability, of poverty, of poor housing, of lack of facilities for young people and lack of care for old people. These were not someone else's problems. They were theirs.

Sharing such stories brings the necessity to be accepting, to own the stories as one's own, to be sensitive in hearing them. It brings the recognition that in hearing someone's story, you are standing on holy ground. For the Urban Theology Group, sharing experience could not do anything but lead to theological reflection. These problems were theirs, as well as the people around them. But they were also God's. They were not alone in their care. God cared too. The ground they were standing on was indeed holy ground, not just as the place of people's deepest hopes and dreams and hurts, but as they place where they met the God who cares.

Gradually, through this sharing and reflecting, the group came to identify a number of themes:

- the importance of their faith, in 'keeping on keeping on.'

- the fact that at times, life was 'a bit of a scunner.'

- the fact that some issues just kept coming up again and again in people's experience; religious bigotry; the lack of attractive options for young people; the effects of unemployment on families; the situation of those on the margins (the frail, the elderly, etc.) whose care was seen as the job of professionals rather than the community.

It was clear that these were issues of particular significance in Orbiston. But how were they being addressed? The fourth fact the group identified was their feeling that the church was not addressing these key issues.

Mapping the Territory

The group continued with the task of looking where they were. Along with the personal mapping, they drew a blank map of the area and tried to fill it in. They drew in bus stops, shops, community centres, schools, and all the other landmarks of their area. When they looked at the full picture, it didn't seem that Orbiston had very much at all in the way of resources or facilities.

At this point, it would have been easy to jump to the conclusion that they had identified the problems, so the next step would be to take some kind of action. But such a jump from experience to action exposed the group to the very real danger of responding to a crisis without giving due consideration to the cause and nature of the problem. They would also run the risk of assuming that the problems or issues identified by a group of 'church people' were actually felt problems or issues within the community as a whole. They had come to a point where they needed more information: in order to check out their own experience and intuition; in order to find out what were the real causes behind these issues.

The work of the Urban Theology Group was entering a new stage. Their theological reflection was leading them back into the community at large, into research and information-gathering. This was not something that was at odds with their faith journey. Latin-American liberation theologian, Leonardo Boff had said that, although the main purpose of theology was God, understanding of God could not replace, or supersede, understanding of justice and oppression in the world.

The theologians of Orbiston were about to ask these basic questions of their community.

3
Hunting for the Truth

The early months of meeting had brought out four key issues the group were focusing on (narrowed down from an initial eight). These categories for initial research were:

- Youth, and the lack of facilities for young people
- Disability, and again the lack of resources
- Unemployment and its impact on the whole community
- Social divisions, especially between Catholic and Protestant

The Urban Theology Group organized itself into four teams, each of which took on the task of research and information gathering on one of these categories. Meetings were initiated with a wide range of organizations and individuals with knowledge and experience in each of the categories. A big task was underway for a small group.

At the same time, aware that possible outcomes of this process might involve expenditure, perhaps of a substantial nature, another small group had been set up, called the Urban Funding Group. It was the task of this group to look into possible sources for funding of projects, and to visit other groups, churches and organizations engaged in similar activities. Little did they know what lay ahead of *them*.

All of this approach was somewhat out of the ordinary for a church group; to others, it did not sound traditionally religious. Neither it was, but in fact, some things were important to hold on to and maintain. All the meetings were begun and ended with worship and prayer. This had been a vital part of the early meetings, as people had shared memories and experiences that were painful, sometimes unhealed. It was to remain vital that the prayer support and nurture continue, as the group members undertook a task that challenged them both practically, in the sheer commitment of time and energy it cost, but also emotionally in confronting their own particular hesitations, biases and preconceived ideas. It was a big step for one group member, for example, to go and interview a head teacher whose office she had only ever been in to be shouted at, as both parent and child. And it was empowering to discover that as a citizen, she had a right to be there to talk about youth provision.

Each small team began by identifying groups and individuals who would have a perspective on the issue being addressed. Meetings were sought, most people agreed to see them, and the teams, working in pairs, began a long series of interviews, each of which was written up. Among those interviewed or contacted were:

Youth Provision

- Headteachers of local secondary and primary schools
- Social Work department
- Children's Panel
- United Neighbours (youth streetwork group)
- Bellshill Information Service for Youth
- YMCA (Orbiston, working with girls)
- YMCA Main Street, Bellshill
- Community Police
- Community Education
- District Councillor
- and young people themselves

Here's one of this group's reports.

Anne had visited the detached youth work project, and although she had initially been uneasy about this, had greatly enjoyed the experience, and had been impressed with what was going on in the area. A group was started in the hut aiming at Assertiveness for girls. It was also hoped to start a First Aid course soon, and a teacher was urgently required. (It was agreed that the group might approach George Bell.) A conference on youth violence was to be held, led by young people, in April. It was suggested that the UTG might quite like to view the Partners in Power video, which had been a catalyst for some of the ongoing detached youth work projects in the town. This was agreed. Other topics which Anne also mentioned were the Skate Posse, and the Groovy Bad Apple Experience. It was noted that there was now less of a problem with solvent abuse among young people, though there was an increasing youth alcohol problem, with children as young as twelve or thirteen drinking 'Buckie' on the street corners.

Anne also raised the issue of a drop-in youth centre in the Orbiston area, which had featured heavily in the local press, and had run into opposition from the local bowling club and other residents in the area. She had written a letter to Richard Lyle, commending him for his efforts, and supporting the venture. Martin also mentioned that he was involved in the support of this project and would be meeting with Bellshill Bowling Club, Richard Lyle and the Community Police the following evening. It was noted that many of the problems about the centre may well derive from the fact that it was to be a District Council centre while detached youth work was funded by the Regional Council.

Catholic/Protestant Divide

Father Brosnan, Priest, St Gerard's RC Church

Mrs Nancy McKenzie, St Vincent de Paul Society, also a partner in a mixed marriage

Mrs Wilma Kennedy, Guide leader

Outreach: school/home liaison group

Local Baptist minister

Orange Order member

Knights of St Columba member

The team had agreed on a number of questions that could be asked at interviews, so that there would be consistency in the process.

1 What do you understand of the history of the Catholic/ Protestant split in Bellshill?

2 As a minister/youth worker/member of organization, etc., what do you think of the Catholic/Protestant split in Bellshill?

3 Although there won't be any difference made by leaders of organizations towards their members, do you encounter any differences made by the members themselves?

4 How do you manage to overcome this?

5 Do you foresee any way in which this rift can be healed?

6 Do you think the churches can/should/will take the lead?

7 Do you think there will be more working together of the churches, rather than unity in, for example, church services?

8 (of mixed marriages) Did you experience much opposition to your marriage from family, friends, church?

9   What reasons did they give?

10 Do you think there would be an advantage in the churches
    of Bellshill working together to help in the community, or
    that it would be more effective were it a group 'from the
    community'?

Here's one of many reports from this group.

Father Brosnan has been in Bellshill for twelve years, and
has seen changes in the Roman Catholic-versus-
Protestant attitude over this time, and in fact over the
last twenty years or so.

The first point he made to us was that as far as ecumenism
or unity is concerned, instead of us all comparing the
differences in the way we worship, we should instead
focus on our common ground, i.e., our belief in Jesus
Christ, and the fact that we are all baptized in His name.

He also stressed his opinion that there is a genuine desire
to come together, and we must all make the effort to meet
and discuss the issues. We must break down the barriers,
but still respect one another.

Do not fear a 'takeover' by another religion.

Don't dwell on the reasons for our differences in the past:
it is the TRUTH that matters.

Young people 'falling away' from the Church: he fears
that young people will be united on a secular rather than
Christian basis.

Adults to blame for many of the problems of youth; i.e.,
drugs sold by adults to younger people, etc., not other
way round.

Don't hide your faith — let younger people see it. But don't go overboard either!

One of the most interesting points noted by the team researching the Catholic/Protestant divide was that the clergy (of whatever persuasion) *all* said sectarianism was not a problem — but none of them would do things together!

Facilities for people with disability

- Motherwell District Council Rent Office
- YMCA, Main St, Bellshill
- Bellshill Cultural Centre
- Windmillhill Day Centre for the mentally ill
- Bellshill Sports Complex
- Hunter Street Workshop
- Social Work Department
- and practically every public building, shop, office, etc., in Bellshill

Here's one of their reports.

June explained that she had not been able to get as much done as she would have liked, mainly because William had been ill. The fact that this is a problem faced by disabled people in general was noted.

She reported that: Munro's have recently got a specially designed taxi for disabled (wheelchair) people; she had contacted Neil Brown about the fact that the phone in the Cultural Centre was impossible for those in a wheelchair to use; that it was hoped that the Sports

Complex would soon be fitted with a hoist for the pool; that the Alhambra Bar was the only bar in the town accessible to those in wheelchairs; and that buildings such as the local churches and post office were not accessible.

Nancy had visited the David Anderson Centre and spoken to Mrs Lennox there. She had discovered that the local branch of Arthritis Care now meets in the centre on the HattonRigg Road. She had also visited Hunter Street and spoken to the officers there (Peter and Agnes). It had been suggested that the group would like to visit the centre again and this time speak to two disabled people using the centre. It was agreed to do this before our next full meeting.

Unemployment

- Unemployment Benefits Office
- Redundancy Project
- District Council
- Employment Training (including researching a number of case studies)
- Youth Training Scheme

Here's one of this team's reports.

I spoke to a young boy who has been on a YTS for eight months and he was disillusioned with it. Initially he felt he would receive a good training, being placed with an electrical contractor. However, apart from the time that he attends Midscot, which was for two weeks every six weeks, he was not getting any training at all, but was just being used as a runabout. Four out of six boys placed with the same firm had already left to go elsewhere for this reason. He quoted one instance where the job was finished and for several mornings they had reported for work only to be kept for a short period and then sent back home again. One morning he arrived to find no workmen there at all — they had been sent to another job, but had not taken the trouble to inform him of this. The YTS boys are paid seventy-five pence per hour and work a thirty-nine hour week. They have to pay the first three pounds travelling expenses themselves.

This firm also takes on 'ET' men — the 'extra tenner' men, who get their unemployment benefit plus an extra ten pounds to do a week's work. These men finish half an hour before the apprentices and the YTS boys.

The group found research in this area particularly dispiriting. They spent a month trying to see someone at the local authority Redundancy Support Unit, and discovered that structures that undermined the ability to communicate at the real point of need.

In Bellshill, they discovered that there was one job vacancy for every twenty-nine people. Prayer on this issue expressed much anger and frustration.

In almost forty interviews, the reports of some of which ran to many pages; in lectures, meetings, much background reading, compiling of data, and in miles of footslogging round Bellshill, the picture of their community was gradually being filled in. And with this clearer picture was growing an understanding, not just of what had happened in Bellshill, but why. Instead of simply lamenting the awful redundancies in the steel industry in North Lanarkshire, the UTG, as people living there and experiencing the drudge of unemployment, began to see the historical and economic forces which lay behind the closures, as well as the social, cultural and moral degeneration which the lack of work brought. This understanding alone was liberating for people — it helped them to feel somewhat less at the mercy of forces they had no control over. But it also was helping them to begin to ask the necessary questions about how to tackle their situation.

By now, it was the spring of 1992. The group had now been going for about eight months. In all of this time, through the sharing of stories, the research and information-gathering, the mapping of their community, their journey and their destination was still an evolving one. In all of this time too, they had been maintaining their link with the Urban Theology Unit in Sheffield, and their prayer and worship life. Though accompanied by the Bible in the journey so far, they had not really gone to it as the main focus of their enquiry. They were about to enter another new stage. But before that, there was one very important thing still to happen. The UTG had to produce a document and a statement for the UTU that reflected back on, and gathered up all the work they had done.

The discussion (or perhaps one might say, struggle) that took place at that meeting is here reproduced in full. It shows very well the seriousness of intent and commitment of this group. It will be very recognizable to many other groups who have struggled in the same way to articulate their knowledge and their reflections on it. It shows how an idea, that of a centre of some description, is labouring to be born.

And, you might say, it is part of what doing theology sounds like.

4
Naming Our Truth

An Urban Theology Meeting

We have got a plan of action for tonight. As Martin explained to you last week, we are going to try to get a Close [statement] document for Martin to take down to Sheffield. First thing we want to do is to get the statement of our problem reflecting back on all the work we have done, so it is putting into our own words what we think the problem is. There are a couple of ways we can do this. As we heard last week, Martin has already said to Sheffield what he has written down, or can we have a rethink, possibly in our wee groups, though there are not many of us tonight. Has anyone got an idea of what we should be looking at?

We are just looking for bits of paper at the moment and then we will discuss ways of getting the rest of it in time. We virtually know what we are going to do but that is not the point.

I think we need to have something that lets us see how big the plan is. There were not that many facilities that were available to us.

What we thought were — problems, and then we can maybe try and stick them together to make a big problem.

So Susan, lack of facilities ...

Well I think in our map of the Orbiston community ...

What about in relation to helping the old?

Are we going to just consider Orbiston?

No.

That is fair enough, but I think what really annoys me was the root of seeing the women suffer.

It was even if they wanted to get the groceries home or in touch with someone from ten to two.

That was only because they were part time and do so many hours a week.

But even the hours the attendants were going to be there they could be away doing something else.

There is not necessarily a lack of commitment on their part, but a lack of commitment further up that they are only putting in something that could not possibly cover.

There is still a lack of communication.

We were not going to be there until five.

Yes, but the department did not come.

They are maybe not taking us seriously.

But whether they said it or not, the promise was that there would be someone out to see us.

A lack of commitment would seem to be quite a major issue in as far as maybe thinking about what happened in the area. There has been a lack of commitment to the area — would that not be fair?

I think that is fair...

I think if there had been a bigger number taking it seriously that would have helped.

Does the lack of communication not just affect them and the other things in the scheme?

I am quite willing to give my expertise to set up the group as long as we could keep it going with volunteers. But could we find the numbers to keep the centre open and the project running?

I am actually thinking of the YMCA ...

Everything is there — all the facilities — all we need is the people.

... is maybe right about the place.

We do not have the money to pay people, so they will need to be volunteers.

People might be committed, but they are committed to lots of things.

What are we trying to solve?

Lack of community support.

What is the object now?

We want to get a statement of what we think should be done.

Why did you not ask us that at the start?

The reason for not asking you that at the start is that it has been said in the past.

I could not remember what it was that he said last week.

(Break)

How do you want to start?

Our Community.

Do you want to mention that it is Orbiston?

We have to say that it is based on Orbiston.

Can you say that the community of Orbiston is lacking the community spirit which can be caused by lack of facilities which is caused by lack of commitment.

I think that that is probably right.

As the result of, or, resulting in ...

If you had community spirit would you have all these things?

I was going to say are the words hope and community spirit always interchangeable? Like, Orbiston lacks hope.

I think that that is very strong — the lack of hope.

Does the community spirit not come when people feel that there is a light at the end of the tunnel and a bit of hope somewhere.

Lack of hope could be very depressing as it is, but that is reality. It is depressing.

Is it the result of high unemployment?

I think in a way this is maybe quite a good part for our box. One of the responses to what we have been hearing about is to suggest community centre sort of places. Now if that is our response to the problem, although we have never actually sat down before and tried to write in one sentence what the problem is, we would probably in our response have a good indication what the problem is and then worked backwards.

Given unemployment and the lack of funding in the area ...

A lot of things do come back to work — I mean unemployment — not always, but money is a big issue.

Changes are needed and needed fast in this community.

They do not care much for Orbiston do they?

Orbiston lacks the community spirit and hope as a result of high unemployment, lack of community commitment and disgust.

I do not know about the last part of it.

You mean from inside?

Or from putting in 'disgust'.

Is the lack of funding for the youth centres a problem?

I think it is conditions that leave them where they are.

I cannot believe there was something about the funding as well.

I do not like how you think that this funding will make them less depressed. It makes it seem as if funding will change their home situation, because it won't, it will only make the facilities provided in the area.

It is lack of funding for facilities for it?

We are just going to end up with a list of problems.

A lack of money in the area, generally, resulted in a community that lacked community spirit.

We would be prepared to say that lack of money in the whole community is the main problem.

I am not sure that it can be, because people with community spirit can be unemployed.

They are all unemployed anyway.

Well there must be something more than just employment.

It cannot just be that they have nothing to do.

I think that community spirit can have money at the root of it as we are all out working during the day, 'chasing the dollar' and we are never in, or have time to speak to our neighbour or that kind of thing, so we do not talk to anyone from that point of view, and that is a local thing. There is no general place for people to meet their neighbours or hang out your washing or for kids to meet except on street corners.

Which they are not allowed to do.

So if they got facilities for that then community spirit would follow.

Community spirit means the community work together and help each other.

My definition is different from that.

It is a personal thing. A lot of people who are generous maybe do not have much hope, but the community spirit is different — people working together or for each other so that the community helps someone.

That is back to hope again.

What Susan was saying — money cannot heal.

If you throw money at them, it probably will.

It will not solve it. It seems to be something to do with the idea of speaking to folk. We just seem to have a waste plan for as far ahead as folk can imagine and, like with you, come the end of the month and you have no money left, you could not say that our situation was without hope, as you know come the beginning of the next month that the money will be in the bank again. It is almost as if it is to do with not really knowing when the next good day within our community is coming. Does that make sense?

Things just ticking along or even keep plodding along.

Plodding along into the groove Monday, Tuesday, etc.

Talking to the kids in the schools, at the end of the day, a vast majority think there will be nothing for them when they leave, so why bother?

Bad employment prospects.

If we can go on to how we are trying to solve the problem — this is just another thought — we are trying to solve the problem by setting up a community facility that at the end of the day is maybe going to take one or two people off the dole queue by employing them, but it is not going to solve the problem of unemployment. While that is perhaps the thing that is causing many of the issues that we are coming up against it is not the problem that we are aiming at, is it? So we have got to try and see the problem that we are trying to solve rather than the problem that is far too big for us. Rather than the lack of hope.

The Summer Mission was the highlight of the holidays.

If we had no age groups then we would have got a lot more people.

If they have the facilities then they would get back the community spirit, but as they do not have the facilities then they do not have the community spirit as they are not working as a community. If there is nowhere for them to work together then there is no community spirit.

Could you have a drop-in centre?

The statement is that everything is related back to the problem of our project.

If we then reduced that part of it, like the community spirit and then rather than collect results we will just leave it.

We could say some factors contributing to this are ... to make sure that this is not the problem stripped down to the bare minimum.

Orbiston lacks community spirit.

You could then go on to say about general lack of communication, etc ...

Make it into a semi-list just say there is a lack of facilities — OK, it might be a bit basic.

The lack of money, communication and hope, surely this is the result of the lack of facilities and community spirit.

Orbiston lacks community facilities and spirit.

I think that that is the main thing. What do you all think?

Can we not make a sentence saying what causes it; what factors are involved?

We do not say that these are only the symptoms.

When we come to solve it we cannot solve the community spirit. Without having the facilities there, you need the facilities to solve the problem of community spirit.

We have to find the solution to that — the problem is lack of community spirit. Our solution is a community centre. To get people to work together.

So it would be in order to say something like, Orbiston lacks community spirit? Or, is it a lack of things for people to do together, true?

I was thinking in relation back to that ...

In the group we can sort the community spirit out.

If we had a facility would that not cover everything?

It is all interrelated and we should not get bogged down trying to say ...

... this is the cause.

Would it not be better to say, 'owing to' rather than 'there are'?

Orbiston lacks community spirit in a way that stands on its own. We could spend an enormous amount saying why it lacks community spirit — some would say money, some would say facilities, some would say high unemployment, some would say there is too much money. All these bits. Years ago, there was a community spirit, with the 'Palace' there was a community spirit, but there was absolutely nothing for anyone there to do.

You made your own entertainment, everybody knew everybody else.

Not many people were working either.

Lack of facilities in the area maybe is not the problem, maybe it is lack of commitment not from the inside but from the outside.

I may be going to cause problems here. The one thing about that is, to date all you have done is to blame outside which suggests that until outside changes we can never change.

We have not put that all the organizations that are in the area feel strangled and held in that area because there is unemployment and a lot of deprivation.

Change it to the area as Martin was saying.

How about the commitment is outside the area?

If you then go on to say that there are inadequate facilities in the area you are making it clear or it seems to me that unless you then have another sentence that talks about perhaps the terminal reasons why there is a lack of community spirit you're really saying, although not in so many words, this lack of community spirit is caused by ...

To have community spirit you have got to have something to be part of the community.

What about when people lived in miners rows — they all had work in common.

They all had something in common.

People now do not work together, they work outside the area, so they now more than ever need something to give them something in common.

We would advise that a place should be made available for people to meet.

I think the answer is that we have to provide facilities.

Could we say that community spirit could be improved by providing a community centre?

The answer comes further down.

We have got a statement of what the problem is.

Orbiston lacks heart.

Orbiston lacks a community.

Who wants to build one?

That would be a lot easier!

Orbiston lacks community spirit and heart caused by there being nowhere for people to meet together and spend time together.

No place for people to meet and get to know others.

Orbiston lacks community spirit through this.

Orbiston lacks community spirit in part because there is no common meeting place.

I think all of those things are implicit in that kind of thing that we have come up with.

Could you say, Orbiston lacks community spirit (new sentence). This is caused in part by ... I think that is quite strong, just, Orbiston lacks community spirit. Just leave it on its own as the first sentence.

Orbiston lacks community spirit. This is caused in part because there is no common meeting place.

This is partly caused by ...

Orbiston lacks community spirit. This is caused in part by ...

No, that is not right.

This is partly caused by ...

Orbiston lacks community spirit. This is partly caused by ...

Do you not think we should expand on that — this is partly caused by ...

We are only trying to solve one of the problems, not all of them.

So that is, like, a very concise statement of the problem as we see it and feel able to tackle it. The first four words are stating the big issue and the next sentence states what we would try to do about it.

Martin, do you have a statement of the problem as you see it?

The one I think I finally went for: 'There is little for people to do together in our community, which lacks a sense of material and spiritual hope.' Which, in a way, I would feel able to say there is little for people to be able to do together in this community which lacks a sense of community spirit. What do you think?

We could have saved ourselves an hour and a half!

5
Reflecting Upon The Word of the Lord

By the spring of 1992, the Urban Theology Group had come a long way. They had told their own stories, and identified in them the areas of suffering, struggle and possibility for their task. They had mapped their area, and identified the facilities and resources — or lack of them — available to people in similar situations. They had done research and spoken to many individuals and organizations to ensure that they were not just generalizing from their own particular contexts, but were grappling with issues that were live and pressing for a great number of people. They had informed themselves as to the causes and effects of these particular issues. And, as the possibility of a Neighbourhood Centre had emerged from their work, they had named their primary task. And it was a big one for a small group of people. They needed to prepare themselves for the journey that lay ahead. They went back to the Bible.

Of course, they had been praying and reading the Bible all the way along. But now the focus of their enquiry shifted from being their situation in Bellshill to being the texts and stories of the Bible. The group began to direct itself to events in the history of the faith which might have points of similarity with their own history and situation. Now there were times when the whole meeting of the group took the form of Bible studies, as they sought greater understanding of their local community in the light of the Word of God. The Old Testament code of law, the early community of the church, many of the miracles and parables of Jesus came alive when read through the light of their own experience.

Here are a couple of examples of the kind of reading they were doing, and the kind of questions they were asking themselves.

Life Issue: Prayer

Jeremiah 29: 1-14
Jeremiah's letter to the Jews in Babylonia

Background: Jeremiah was living in Jerusalem at the time when the city was plundered by the Babylonian Empire, and the leaders forced into exile. Jeremiah has written to those who are living in exile, encouraging them to become fully involved in the life of their local community.

Questions:

1.   Is there ever a temptation to escape from the place where we are living, and to dream a better place for ourselves and our families to stay.

2.   How effectively, and in what ways, can we work for the good of our town? (v. 7)

3.   Is it right to pray for the prosperity of our community? (v. 7)

4.   Is there a danger that we will listen to the false prophets of our own community? (v. 8) What sort of things do these false prophets proclaim? How can we know that they are false in their predictions, rather than those we listen to?

5.   How great is our hope for the future? When good things happen, how often do we spend time thanking God?

6. Is the work we are now undertaking related to a future hope of the future kingdom of God/heaven?

Luke 11: 1-13
Jesus' Teaching on Prayer

Questions:

1. Why did the disciples want Jesus to teach them to pray? How do we pray?

2. In what ways can God's name be honoured?

3. How do we think of the kingdom of God? As something in the future, or as something which we can see parts of in our present life?

4. When we pray, do we ever ask for too much? Is it sufficient simply to ask for what we will need each day, or do we ask for more?

5. Do we seek forgiveness for our own failings before we complain about the faults of others? What would be the consequence of adopting such an attitude?

6. Do we pray not to have times of hard testing, or rather that once we are in such times that the pain will be taken away from us?

7. Can we think of a modern example of vs 5 - 8? Are we ever ashamed to ask and to keep asking God for something?

8. Have vs 9 - 10 been our personal experience with regard to prayer? If so, can we share some

example? If not, how can we begin to explain why not?

9. What are some of the good things which our Father in heaven has given to us through the course of our lives, and over recent years?

Life Issue: Sharing

Questions:

1. How many examples of sharing can we think of within the Bible?

2. In what ways is our Project about sharing?

Acts 2: 43 - 47
Life among the believers

Questions:

1. What sort of miracles would fill people with a sense of awe today? Is the church still capable of performing 'miracles and wonders'?

2. Are close fellowship and the sharing of belongings possible activities for the church of today? How might fellowship be strengthened? Do we share enough of our belongings with one another as individuals? As a church?

3. Do we think that the members of the early Christian community just shared with one another, or did their sharing go further afield?

4. Is worship purely a Sunday event? What are the advantages of meeting for daily worship?

5. Why do people not share meals now to the same extent as happened in the past?

6. Was the adding to their number on a daily basis as a result of a strategy for mission, or as a result of genuine Christian living?

Acts 4: 32 - 37
The believers share their possessions

Questions:

1. What does it mean to be 'one in mind and heart'? Is this something which is achievable?

2. Do we tend to seek praise for what we give and do for others and for the church?

3. Why did the apostles have such great power to witness to the resurrection of Jesus?

4. Do we distribute our goods according to the needs of people, rather than according to their capabilities?

A number of passages were particularly important to the group as they travelled onwards on their journey of discovery.

Jeremiah 31: 13-15

A vision of a community where girls dance with happiness, and men, old and young alike, rejoice; where all the needs of the people are met. This passage goes on to speak of the sound of a mother weeping bitterly for her children' ...they are gone, and she refuses to be comforted...'

Psalm 42

One of the great songs of exile, and of calling out to God, '... why have you forgotten me? Why must I go on suffering?..'

Lamentations 3: 18 - 24

A lament of suffering and hope '... the Lord is all I have, and so I put my hope in him ...'

Romans 15: 1 - 6

' ... we who are strong in the faith ought to help the weak to carry their burdens ...'

2 Corinthians 4: 8

'... we are often troubled, but not crushed; sometimes in doubt, but never in despair ...'

Matthew 20: 1 - 16

The parable Jesus told about the workers in the vineyard ... 'so those who are last will be first, and those who are first will be last.'

Matthew 7: 1 - 12

From the Sermon on the Mount, '... do not judge others, so that God will not judge you ...' ...'ask, and you will receive, seek, and you will find, knock and the door will be opened to you ...'. '... Do for others what you want them to do for you; this is the meaning of the Law of Moses and the teachings of the prophets.'

1 Corinthians 12: 12 - 26

'Christ is like a single body with many parts ... if one part of the body suffers, all the other parts suffer with it; if one part is praised, all the other parts share its happiness.'

Ecclesiastes 3: 1 - 8

A time for everything under heaven.

Struggle and Encouragement

In the course of this reflecting on the Word of the Lord, members of the group found themselves amazed. In a way they were 'brainstorming the Bible'. They discovered that Paul had written a lot about religious bigotry. In the Creation story, they found a story of God at work — and then resting, pleased with the work. So to deny someone the right to work was a denial of part of the image of God in them. In the story of the workers hired in the marketplace to work in the vineyard, they saw the job centre of the first century. These workers, like twentieth-century workers, needed a job because they needed the money — and their needs were the same, whether they had a job or not, whether they were new on the job or not!

But they found that the Bible didn't only speak to and of their own history and context. It didn't only speak to and of their own suffering and hope and vision. It also spoke to and of their ongoing struggles. George MacLeod, the Founder of the Iona Community, itself born out of the struggles of the Depression in Glasgow, wrote, 'prayer refreshes on the knife-edge.' The Urban Theology Group was being driven back again and again to the Bible, and to prayer, because they were on the knife-edge.

They had never expected it to be easy — and perhaps they had never expected it to be so *big!* But they were having to face a number of significant problems.

In their data-gathering, there was a real problem of getting hard information which was up-to-date and referred to their area. To give one example; the 1981 Census was hopelessly out of date, and even the Voluntary Population Survey (Strathclyde Region 1986) was very outdated. The 1991 Census figures would not be available locally until Spring 1993, and even they would already be inaccurate. The Census had been carried out a month before the closure of one of the major steel works, and since the Census, over 3000 jobs had gone with the closure of Clydesdale Tube Works and Ravenscraig alone.

In the ongoing life of the Urban Theology Group, there was a problem with absenteeism and keeping people informed. This was as the result of personal circumstances such as ill health and family crises. The fact that people in the group continued to experience hardship contributed to the high quality of understanding that existed when dealing with community issues (nothing could ever get too theoretical without being brought down to earth) but it meant that it was hard to keep the flow of information going for people who unavoidably missed meetings.

And the meetings themselves were always in danger of being swamped by the sheer quality and quantity of work being undertaken by group members. There was simply so much to feed back, to discuss, to collate, to reflect on. The meetings were getting longer and longer.

Perhaps because of this weight of work and length of meetings, the time of prayer and worship built into every meeting had to guard against turning stale and formulaic, as opposed to being a catalyst for what was happening.

And, as in every group, there were issues of group dynamics — did some people dominate while others were reluctant to speak up? And how to address this problem?

And always, reading the Bible through the lens of Orbiston,

new questions were being raised, new challenges sighted, new insights gained, but almost too fast to be absorbed fully. It was a bit like doing theology on the run. (Though it should be added that one evening, when Martin raised doubts as to whether the group was going too fast, another member said to him, 'Martin. We believe that this is what God wants us to do. If you don't like it, you can get out, but we're going to try it anyway.' That's telling your minister what's what!)

The relationship with the Urban Theology Unit in Sheffield, and Martin's participation in the Master in Ministry course had been intended to help with all these issues, and to provide a framework for addressing them. But this was not turning out to be the case, and in fact, the relationship was in danger of turning into one more of the problems. Though appreciating the resource of the UTU, and the personal contacts made, more and more the course requirements were sitting uneasily with the local requirements in Orbiston. There were getting to be too many occasions when the group had to shelve some worthwhile piece of local work in order to complete course work (some of which seemed to have little bearing on the whole project). A resource which should be a useful servant was at risk of becoming an unhelpful master, and in fact, to cease to be the liberative methodology it sought to be.

Nor did it look as if the conflict of work pressures between the Urban Theology Group in Orbiston and the Urban Theology Unit in Sheffield was going to get any easier in the near future. If any funding was to be sought from the Urban Aid programme for a possible centre, a submission would need to be made in the summer of 1993 — a considerable task. Such a timescale seemed impossible to match with the requirements of the course. But many conversations needed to be held in the meantime before such a submission could be made. Given the Urban Theology Unit's project requirements, and the uncertainty of the Orbiston project, it seemed all the more inappropriate for the relationship to continue. Given the choice, the local group elected to go on with its own work rather than follow the work of the Urban Theology Unit.

Many struggles, indeed, and the group needed all the encouragement it could get, from prayer and Scripture, from each other, and from supportive friends. But it was not all problem. Small things were beginning to happen.

6
Responding in Grace to the Task

Almost without realizing it, members of the group were beginning to be drawn into action on a number of issues. These included plans to install phones accessible to disabled people in the local library/cultural centre, and being contacted by the local YMCA regarding the development of disabled facilities in their premises. The little ripples the Urban Theology Group had started by their interest in access for people with disability had begun to spread across a bigger pool.

Then there was the successful campaigning in support of plans to build a local youth centre. The group was represented at public meetings where opposition was being expressed to such a centre. At one of the meetings, a letter from a UTG member was read out by a local district councillor, comparing the attitude of those who opposed the building to that of the priest and the Levite who walked by one the other side in the story of the Good Samaritan. It wasn't that they were bad people; the priest and the Levite, just that they were busy with their own concerns, and had no room for something that interfered with their own interests. The opposers to the youth centre withdrew their opposition. And while the local community awaited the building of the new centre, some members of the UTG were keen to see if there was any way in which an interim facility could be offered.

These small achievements were having a big effect on the group. They had begun to believe in their power to change things, to make things happen. It gave them confidence for bigger things. Much bigger things! Now they were in a different place. Their journey had moved them on.

Their naming of the reality of their local community ('Orbiston lacks a sense of community. This is, in part, caused by the lack of a common meeting place.') was bringing them closer and closer to home. Where was there a building that might be utilized, that might act as the youth centre's interim facility. They began to think about the underused buildings in the area. They began to think about their own church building!

Here was a building, Orbiston Parish Church, right in the heart of the community, that was massively underused. Could *it* be adapted, renovated, even built on to, in order that the church itself might try to become part of the solution to the problem they had identified. It was clear that this was a major proposal, that, if it were to go ahead, would require the approval, not just of the group, or even the kirk sessions, which had been kept informed about the progress of the group. It would require the support of the whole church.

Sharing the Knowledge

A congregational meeting, to which all the members of both Orbiston and Saint Andrew's churches were invited, was arranged for October 1992. The plans for this important church meeting were carefully made. Clearly, people should be given as much information as possible, not just about the proposal, but about the process that had led to it. It was decided that the meeting should include the following:

- the information to be given 'step-by-step', starting with motivation, i.e. a Christian response to a need within the community, and how that need was identified.

- information gathered over the past year to be relayed, and ideas for later discussion put forward.

- explanation of the subsequent stages of development if the project is given the go-ahead: surveys; final proposals to congregations; follow-up meetings, etc.

- involvement of two separate groups should be stressed:

  the Urban Aid Group (elders from both churches);

  the Urban Theology Group (members from both congregations)

- speakers from groups (both Christian and secular) who have been successful in establishing Urban Aid projects to be invited along to talk about their experiences, and to be briefed on their input beforehand.

- a question/answer session to be held *after* the presentation;

- no discussion during the event to avoid being sidetracked.

- a questionnaire to be circulated at the end of/during the evening.

- no mention to be made of current Parish Reappraisal (a Church of Scotland national analysis of parochial needs and resources), unless requested, as outcome not able to be predicted. If raised, however, the point to be made that the Reappraisal Committee will take any project into account, so it is possible to carry on without reference to this separate issue.

- the presentation to be conducted on a 'worship' basis, consistent with the style of the Urban Theology Group meetings.

Mention should also be made of the fact that in order for the project to succeed, full co-operation from both Orbiston *and* St Andrew's Churches would need to be secured.

At this meeting, which asked for permission and approval to go ahead and explore this possibility, a secret ballot was held. Despite clear concern expressed by some, there was a massive majority in favour of going ahead.

Starting All Over Again

The Urban Theology Group now had a number of things it didn't have when it started. It had:

- a clear idea of the issues facing their community, and of the social, political and economic factors that shaped these.

- a vision for a better life for their community, which had been confirmed and encouraged by the many groups and organizations whose opinions they had sought

- deepened roots in their own prayer life, Scriptures and faith.

- a new confidence in their ability to change things, based on some small but significant achievements

- a practical proposal to put their own resources at the service of their community and their vision, backed almost unanimously by the membership of their churches.

They had indeed come a long way. They were in a new situation. And like any new situation, this one required research, information-seeking, opinion-testing. Once again, almost without realizing it, they were hunting for the truth. In what has been termed the *spiral* of liberation theology, they were following a process which is like a circle, except that it ends up in a different place.

In that different place, the sharing of experiences, the quest for understanding, the reflection on the Word of God, and the practical action is a process of *doing* theology, which is not interested just in thinking about God in the world, but in acting in solidarity with God in *changing* it.

It's an activity not just of information, or even of reformation, but of transformation; a change from oppression to freedom, from poverty to sufficency, from isolation to community. Seen in this light, it is a liberating theology.

7
An Idea Worth Exploring

Knocking on the doors

The idea of a neighbourhood centre based in Orbiston Parish Church, open to all, and offering the possibility of rediscovering some of the lost spirit of community was by now firmly established. But once again, the Urban Theology Group had to ask itself hard questions. Was this just a pipe dream? Was it feasible? And did it really address many of the problems they had identified? Was it what people really wanted?

The best way to find that out was to ask them. But what would be the best way to do that? There were organizations and groups — but they represented different age groups, different interests in the community. In the end, they decided upon the simplest method. They would go out, knock on doors, street by street, and ask people in their community what they thought about this idea. To help this process, they decided to draw up a questionnaire which they would ask people to fill in and return.

Going out in groups of two once again, they decided to visit every other house in the parish — a total of six hundred houses. Their questionnaire was drawn up with the assistance of CAVOC (Community and Voluntary Organisations Council). Remembering that when Jesus did mission, he asked more questions than he answered, they were back out on the streets again. They were going with a biblical understanding of community, interested in and concerned not just for the people who shared their convictions or lifestyle — the people they liked

— but for the whole community. In a time when individualism was part of the political philosophy of the day, had taken root, but had paralysed people, the solutions to the fractures of community could not be found in sectarianism of any kind.

Of course they were nervous about this big task, and about the kind of responses they would meet. Would there be hostility, apathy, resentment of the church? In fact, they were to be pleasantly surprised by the very good responses they got at the doors. There was much enthusiasm for the idea of a neighbourhood centre, and again and again, stress laid on the need for something for young people in particular. Part of the questionnaire asked about people's involvement in a possible centre — would they use it, would they consider volunteering in it? Again, the responses were positive. They received four hundred completed questionnaires.

The data on the questionnaires, and from the doorstep conversations, was incorporated into the developing plans for the centre. Clearly, there was widespread local support for the idea. Concerns raised — about things like noise disturbance, problems about car-parking, were addressed and answered. Questions were asked about the kind of activities people would be interested in seeing in the centre.

Now that there was the kind of community affirmation they sought for the centre, and with a clearer idea of what such a centre should contain, it was time to take the next step, and find an architect who would be interested in drawing up plans for such a building. When taking soundings to find a suitable firm, the group found that there were lots of firms sympathetic to the ethos of the project. The final decision was made in favour of a Glasgow firm, and Bill Watson became the project architect.

At a second congregational meeting in April 1993, the results of the survey were shared with the whole membership of the two churches. The architect had brought some provisional plans, and people were invited to make comments, suggestions and choices about them. Once again, the emphasis was on giving people information, options, choices and the opportunity to say no. It was on giving them power. Asked to vote again, on the question, 'is this a form of mission', the vote was overwhelmingly in favour of going ahead.

The project was now well on its way. But it was becoming clear that a number of decisions about organization and management structure needed to be taken. At a final congregational meeting in June 1993, the two churches, voting separately so that it would be clear whether the support came from *both* of them, voted to set up a charitable company. This would have its own board of directors. No longer would the project be controlled by the congregational board of the churches. They would hand over control to this board of directors. The board would consist of local people, (including five of the nine nominated on an annual basis by the kirk session of Orbiston Church) at an AGM. And, in a move which was surprising to many, given the sectarian history of the area, the board would be ecumenical.

Because of their step-by-step journey, the surprise remained surprise, and was not hostility. But here was a group from two churches who had done all this hard work. It would have been no surprise if they had wanted to retain control of it. It would have been no surprise if St Andrew's Church had chosen to opt out at this point — after all, though their parish, it was not *their* building which would be served. It would have been no surprise if they had wanted to keep it a strictly Presbyterian affair.

The congregational vote in favour of the new company and its status was unanimously in favour. And wise decisions they proved to be. Catholic members of the board and subsequently the staff have been worth their weight in gold. And members from St Andrew's have shown a commitment to the project which has been imaginative and selfless. Without their commitment, the project could not have gone ahead. When unions and linkages are so often in the news because of arguments, splits, divisions and territorial manoeuvring, it is inspirational to see what can be done when being a good neighbour is practised by churches as well as individuals.

Utheo Ltd was established in July 1993. (Guess where the name came from! It's a contraction of urban theology.) But even before this could happen, the money had to be raised to pay for its granting of charitable status. An arts and crafts fair was held to raise the money — the first fund-raiser of many!

Many doors had already opened to their knocking. But there were many doors still to be knocked on-and the next big one was the money door. During the summer of 1993, an Urban Programme application was prepared and submitted. It was the big one, but over the course of the next year, more than seventy separate funding applications were made.

To begin with, the noises were not encouraging. 'Don't be stupid!' (chief executive) ... 'too ambitious' ... 'amateurs trying to be professionals' ... were only a few of the comments they received. But gradually, the quality of their work, the thoroughness of their grounding, and the integrity of their commitment began to impress people. The first real breakthrough came when the Lanarkshire Development Agency promised £30,000 in partnership funding. This was serious money! At that point, according to one of the Group, 'we really began to believe we could do it.'

To further their fundraising, and also because interest in the project was beginning to grow from outside the area, members of the group and of Utheo (some of whom were the same) began to take on public speaking engagements, travelling to visit churches, agencies and local authorities in many different places. Some of these meetings were for the purpose of fine-tuning the plans for the centre, for building partnership arrangements for the services it would offer, and to keep working with local groups and organizations. And people who were quite unused to public speaking, or negotiating contracts found that they were developing a whole new range of skills and confidence.

Throughout the autumn and winter of 1993 into 1994, the Urban Theology Group continued to meet, and to receive reports from Utheo.

Here are the minutes of a few of these meetings.

28 November 1993

Present: Martin, Susan, Anita, Nancy, Jim, Shirley, Evelyn, Annabelle.

Opening reading by Anita: Romans 12: 10

Utheo news:

a.   Strathclyde Regional Council have given £500 towards administration costs.

b.   The Tudor Trust have donated £30,000.

c.   Agreement by group to give a gift to Lawrie Taggart's secretary for her assistance with our Urban programme application.

d.   The group agreed to send Christmas cards to everyone who has been of help to our project.

Tonight's theme: Communities and the Bible

a.   Disciples

b.   Children of Israel

c.   Rebuilding of Jerusalem

d.   Noah and family

e.   Joseph and family

f.   Communities of this century

Closing reading by Anita: 1 Corinthians 13: 1 - 7

Prayer

9 December 1993

Present: Martin, Susan, Anita, Jim, Evelyn, Ann, Annabelle

Opening reading by Annabelle: Hebrews 3: 1 - 6

Utheo news:

a. ALC meeting confirmed our Urban Programme application has gone to the Scottish Office as highest supported for the region. Barbara Philben suggested that we should write to them and the Scottish Office if we have to reduce grant.

b. Levi Strauss phoned about possible contribution of £3856 for furniture for daycare project. We have to confirm when we have building started.

c. Major Trust Funds applications have been completed at 76.

Tonight's Theme: Communities and the Bible

a. Disciples — communed together

    Children of Israel - Exodus, Leviticus 19: 33 - 37, Numbers

Theme for future meeting: Book of Nehemiah

Closing reading by Annabelle: Isaiah 25: 1

Prayer

3 January 1994

Present: Martin, Susan, Anita, Evelyn, Nancy, Annabelle

Opening reading by Martin

Utheo news:

a.   £3000 has been received from Robertson Trust

b.   £15,000 has been agreed by the Congregational
       Board from proposed sale of land at Orbiston to
       Neighbourhood Centre.

c.   LDA meeting have confirmed grants for £35,000
       for outdoor work and £2500 towards architect's
       fees.

d.   Children in Need organizer phoned saying that
       after reading our synopsis and other
       information, he thought what we are offering is
       very well thought-out, and has agreed to give us
       his support if it is put before the trustees.

e.   Iain Johnston, area officer, Urban Priority Fund
       of the Church of Scotland has asked if we will
       arrange a Thanksgiving Service at Orbiston.

We have agreed to this service on Thursday 17 March at 6 p.m.
on the theme of our spiral: Experience
                                     Exploration
                                     Reflection
                                      Response

Prayer: Martin

Progress was being made on other fronts. Community Enterprise had agreed to run a weekly surgery within the Centre. The Careers Service agreed to run regular surgeries within the Centre. The Social Work Department had agreed to be the sponsoring body for the Project, and felt that if revenue funding was not forthcoming from the Urban Programme application, they could pay for some of the revenue costs.

It was a busy time! And by anybody's standards, a demanding one, being lived by a group of people who were doing this in their spare time, and who had no professional qualifications for any of it; only the deep knowledge of a place and a people that comes from living in it, and loving them.

Not only was it busy, it also had its own struggles, problems and disappointments. One of the things that was hardest for the Urban Theology Group to bear was the fact that opposition and obstacles, which might have been expected from those outside the church, had in fact come predominantly from within the church — never locally, but in its regional and national structures and institutions. So difficult had some of these negotiations been (at the points at which local Church of Scotland churches have to operate within constraints laid down by the Church at presbyterial and General Assembly level) that one minute of that period, to do with the formation of the limited company, has a positively revolutionary and subversive tone to it on the part of the UTG! As Martin wrote ruefully,

'Perhaps the conservative structures of the established church make progress and change, with the inevitable risks involved, particularly hard.'

They needed their recourse again and again to the Bible, and to the stories of faith communities in different parts of the world, such as El Salvador, and to their shared prayer, to encourage one another through these difficulties, to the point where they could affirm:

'Through difficult times, we have struggled on knowing that all of us, albeit from very different perspectives, are about, is the building up of God's kingdom.'

And indeed, the doubters were gradually won round to full support.

Nor were they lacking in encouragement from many in the church. Encouragement came from the elder in Drumchapel (a Glasgow housing scheme) who advised them very early on to 'keep hold of the vision'; from many who had travelled similar paths of suffering, struggle and empowerment; from the people who prayed for them; from those who invited them to share their story with the wider church; and most of all from the local people.

In all of this support, in fact, in the course of the whole journey so far, they had discovered that God was involved in the whole of their lives. They had found that prayer was life-giving and refreshing. The place of prayer and fellowship within their group had been central in enabling them to 'keep on keeping on' (to quote Martin Luther King) during the most difficult times. Without the powerhouse of prayer and the blessing of God's Spirit, they believed, they could have accomplished nothing.

In May 1994, they received the answer to their Urban Programme application. They had been awarded £165,000! The stiffest door had swung open. Now, they had an idea whose time had come.

8
'Behold, I Make All Things New'

New Centre

By the end of 1994, tenders for the work had gone out, and building was about to begin. This was a description of the centre which the builders would be constructing.

'The Neighbourhood Centre will be based within the buildings of Orbiston Parish Church. It will be non-denominational and open to everyone in the area, with full disabled access. A new wing is being built to the west of the existing premises, replacing a derelict wooden hut. The capital costs of the project are £270,000, and revenue costs are in the region of £120,000 per annum. Through a wide range of local and national agencies, the complete capital and revenue costs have been met for an initial four-year period.

The supervising body for the project during its initial phase is the Social Work Department of Strathclyde Regional Council. The management committee is a charitable company limited by guarantee, set up specifically to develop and manage the Centre. (Company name: Utheo Ltd. Company No. 145454, Scottish Charity No. SCO21687). Utheo Ltd, founded in July 1993 intends to develop key aspects of the project as a community business, run by local community members and employing local people. Any profits made from the trading arms would require to be spent on the provision of better services and employment opportunities for the people of Orbiston. In this way the Centre will seek to promote economic as well as social, environmental and spiritual improvement within the area.

Orbiston Neighbourhood Centre will aim to be a multi-purpose and multi-functional resource for the whole Orbiston area. The Centre will seek to promote integration among groups using the centre, and to break down the existing social, generational and religious divisions. It will aim to develop and foster a sense of community and worth within the Orbiston APT (Area of Priority Treatment).

The Centre will provide a wide range of activities in keeping with its primary objectives. These will include: daycare provision for up to twenty vulnerable and isolated elderly per day: Youth Club facilities (up to twenty on any occasion): Latch Key Club (maximum twenty-five): Play Group and Parents and Toddlers (maximum eighteen): All-Day Café (the only one in Orbiston) and a Lunch Club (maximum seating of twenty). There will be a daily worship service for any wishing to attend, and a quiet room for private prayer and meditation. In addition, part of the main hall will be available for soft recreational activities (carpet bowls, etc.), and for a clothes exchange and food co-operative, when not being used for other activities. Money advice, benefits advice, job search and careers facilities, as well as a basic pastoral counselling resource will be available within the building. The targeting of these specific services is the result of careful analysis regarding the particular needs of the local area.

The project will employ five full-time and three part-time members of staff, and it is intended to develop further employment opportunities as the work of the Centre is developed. At the same time, the Centre will rely heavily on volunteer staff, and an extensive pool of volunteers has already been established. The use of volunteers within the Centre is a deliberate policy to encourage local people to become the providers as well as the recipients of services, thus promoting a greater sense of community.

The project is one of the most innovative and imaginative underway at the present time. In seeking to develop an amenity which is funded through both private and public sector funding, one which will be income-generating through the provision of necessary services, and one in which local people are empowered to become volunteers, employees and members of the company, the Centre is seeking to provide a holistic approach to the complex set of problems facing the community of Orbiston and similar communities.'

Work began in January 1995, and its progress was marked and accompanied by prayer in the monthly Prayer Letter of the Orbiston Neighbourhood Centre; a letter begun in February 1995 by Annabelle Stewart, the Utheo Company Secretary, and still continuing. The daily prayer entries make illuminating reading, giving as they do a flavour both of the practical, small details of building, *and* of the breadth of vision which had accompanied the project all along.

March 1

Pray that all the work for the Centre enhances God's service in the community.

March 2

Pray that the site meeting taking place today fails to uncover any problems.

March 3

Pray for the needs of those who suffer injustice and deprivation, and for those who work to provide for the basic needs of others.

March 4

Thank God for his guidance in our lives, and when things get difficult may his Spirit renew us.

March 5

Give thanks to God for the sharing of services at St Andrew's whilst Orbiston is under reconstruction.

March 6

Pray that the Safety Survey by Orbiston A.L.C. will improve conditions in the area.

March 7

Pray for Father Gustavo Gutierrez, a Brazilian priest who is recognized as being the founder father of the Liberation Theology Movement upon which much of our Urban Theology Group has depended. He will start a three-day series of lectures at Stirling University today.

March 8

Give thanks for £3500 donation towards Worship Co-ordinator's salary.

March 9

Pray that John, Jim and Hazel manage the employment details with ease.

March 10

Pray that the tickets for a fundraising dance will be sold.

The building was completed in August 1995. Only just, for the opening date was 4 August, and on 3 August there was still an army of subcontractors finishing off jobs (and in the way of these things, some of them were still being completed several weeks on.) But enough was finished; this was a transformed building. Already, the Saturday before the day of the official opening, there had been an Open Day, with activities for children and adults alike, when local people had a chance to satisfy their curiosity. Another Summer Mission Team from Aberdeen had done a house-to-house delivery round the area with information about the Centre, and invitations to come and see it and use it.

The opening was to be a great event. It was to be performed by the Moderator of the General Assembly of the Church of Scotland, Rt Revd James Harkness, and the Roman Catholic Bishop of Motherwell was to take a leading part in the opening ceremony. There would be many invited guests — friends, supporters, people who had worked on the project — and of course, it would be open to the people of Orbiston, and the wider Bellshill area. There would be party food, and a chance to look at and admire the new building. There would be a photographic record of the building. In the evening, there would be a special Songs of Praise act of worship held in thanksgiving.

4 August 1995 was a glorious day. The sun shone, the sky was blue, and everything went according to plan. Hundreds of people were present from church and community, and from much further afield in Scotland. The mood was joyful, celebrative ,and, for not a few people, filled with relief that they were in a state to open. For the members of Orbiston and Saint Andrew's churches, and perhaps in particular for the people who had worked so long and so hard to bring this vision to fulfilment, there was satisfaction, gratitude, and a sense of wonder that their journey, often uphill and full of difficulty,

had brought them this far. It was an occasion for best outfits, much picture-taking, laughter, song and heartfelt thanksgiving. Above all, it was an occasion for new hope. At the Songs of Praise, the Moderator preached on the story of the Good Samaritan. He could not have chosen better.

Not that the pressure had let up at all. As well as the final mad rush to be ready for the opening, Susan Johnstone, Martin's wife, had given birth to their second son, David, just a few days earlier.

And there were tears among the laughter and song; tears of release and rejoicing, yes, but also tears of sadness and loss. After a long and valiant struggle with illness, John Bowman, whose vision and commitment and sense of humour had meant so much, and had kept people going through the worst of times, died just before the opening, leaving a widow, Sheena, and a young son, Andrew. At the opening ceremony, his favourite hymn was sung: 'Shine, Jesus, Shine'. When they came to sing the line that goes, *'Mirrored here, may our lives tell your story'*, many people had John in their hearts. Though he did not live to see the fruits of his labour, his spirit was present throughout that whole great day. And Sheena has continued the family involvement by working as a volunteer in the Centre.

At the Songs of Praise, during prayers of thanksgiving and concern led by people from Bellshill churches of several denominations, symbols of the work and hopes of the Centre were brought forward and laid on a table, and prayers were offered for the many different groups of people who were now part of its life. Not now just the Urban Theology Group and the members of Orbiston and Saint Andrew's, now there were *staff* who worked in the Centre day by day.

New Staff

The first person to be appointed to the staff was the centre manager, Irene Gibson. Living in nearby Rutherglen, and a member of the church Martin had worked at in Castlemilk, Irene had a background in catering and management, and a wealth of practical experience which was to stand her in good stead in the new venture. But more importantly, she has the kind of personality which combines attention to detail, the ability to keep her head when all around her are panicking, and the gift of making everyone feel genuinely welcomed and wanted.

She was soon joined by several more staff members. Caretaker David Fox had worked for the BBC, where he learned the ability to fix everything which was to be so important, and lived conveniently across the road for his keyholding duties. Dorothy Bright, the secretary, could read everyone's writing, and made order out of the sheaves of paper that descended from everywhere, as well as paying the wages. She may well be the only person who knows where everything is. Dorothy belongs to a Pentecostal fellowship.

John Groome was appointed to the vital position of centre cook — a big change, since his last job had been at Ravenscraig, the nearby steel plant which had recently closed with huge job losses and the inevitable consequences of these. John's cooking, delicious, healthy, affordable, and introducing customers to many new culinary delights, was indeed to prove so popular that both the café and the lunch-club soon became over-subscribed, and plans are now afoot to build an extension to the café (which uses and advertises fairly-traded products). But as important in creating a welcoming atmosphere in the cafe have been John's warm personality and creative temperament, and he is a favourite with all the ladies in the daycare service. John is a Roman Catholic.

Marion McCready is a member of the local RC church, and a resource worker in the daycare service. Norma Russell, the organist in Orbiston Church, is also a resource worker, and the first senior resource worker was Elizabeth Keddie, a member of the Congregational church. The care, sympathetic attention and genuine interest of these three staff members was a key reason in the increasing success of the daycare service, which now provides an invaluable community resource, and has, quite literally, transformed the lives of a number of elderly people who hitherto had been isolated and housebound.

The last staff member appointed at the time of opening was Kathy Galloway, as Worship and Counselling Co-ordinator. She was appointed to develop the daily, ecumenical act of worship, which would be led by staff, volunteers and users of the Centre. With a fixed-term appointment of one year, she also organized basic counselling and befriending training for staff and volunteers, and worked with groups planning ecumenical worship throughout the year in the Bellshill area. Her last task for the Centre has been to write this book.

This was the group which opened the doors of the Centre on the first full day of operation, and waited for the general public to rush in! Well, maybe not. Nothing happens quite like that. For the first few weeks, few people came around. The daycare referrals of elderly people was being held up by administrative difficulties in the social work department. Word had not yet got around about the café. Things were slow.

But gradually, step by step, things happened. The first group of elderly people arrived, looking around them nervously. Different community groups began to ask to use the building. A few single people, a few families, began to lunch regularly in the café. Visitors began to wander in, kids began to come around. There began to be a bit of a buzz. The centre was on its way. We should have known that this is the way it would be-step by step, one foot and then the next, not quite knowing where we were g1oing. This is the way it had been all along.

As time went on, and the work expanded, the staff did too. Janis Scott was appointed as trainee, then assistant cook. Anne Forbes came to share the senior careworker (daycare) job. And work with children and young people began. Paul Youngson, a stalwart of the local YMCA was appointed as Senior careworker (out-of-school care), and was joined by Sam McAleer and Linda Quince as careworkers. Now the Centre could offer after-school care facilities and youth work to children and young people in the area. And Margaret Hawthorn was appointed as volunteer co-ordinator, to develop and expand this important aspect of the centre's life. Thirteen members of staff from a variety of backgrounds, nearly all local, and, most importantly, a staff which is ecumenical, breaking down barriers of sectarianism. Since then the staff has continued to change and grow.

New Volunteers

The presence of volunteers also helped to break down barriers.

At the time of the survey, local people had been invited to volunteer, to assist in the café, in the daycare, in working with young people, and this invitation had been followed up at a number of public meetings before the centre opened. They too have been a diverse group; from different churches, and of different ages, from teenagers to some whose years could match the people in daycare — but whose energy, enthusiasm and commitment would shame many a twenty-year old. Judging by them, one would get the impression that Bellshill must be full of older people, mostly women, but including some men, whose range of interests, as well as their own families and volunteering, cover everything from classes in pottery to aerobics for the over-fifties. You get the feeling that if you suggested that they might like to try parachuting out of an aeroplane, they would jump at the suggestion; the vision of the Orbiston Skydiving Grannies Team is irresistible!

Their number has been added to at various times by students on community care placements from nearby Motherwell College. And the most far-travelled volunteers to date have been a young couple from India, in Scotland on World Exchange, an international volunteer programme of the Scottish churches. Praveen Frederick and his wife Mary (known to all as Fred and Mary) from the state of Kerala in South India, spent nearly a year living in a flat in Orbiston, and working in the Centre. Though there were many cultural differences to face, Praveen wrote about their time in Orbiston:

> 'Working in the Orbiston Neighbourhood Centre has helped us a great deal to associate with the local community here, and we have many happy memories to treasure. The broad smile of one of our friends in the elderly daycare when we help her in the activities; the pains the church members took in equipping our flat (heavy furniture was shifted to the top floor with smiling faces); the friendship and fellowship we enjoyed among the Orbiston church members with occasional tea sessions; the waving hands and the call, 'Fred' by the small kids; the newsagent from Pakistan who hands over my 'Scottish Daily Express' and the small talk over the counter; the tasty Chicken Jaipuri from the local 'Spice of Kashmir' ... the attachments are long.'

The volunteers bring a dimension that is spiritual as well as practical. They clear dishes in the café-but they also have time just to sit and chat to people in the daycare when the staff are busy, to share reminiscences and listen to stories, to sympathize about family problems and to help harassed young parents with energetic toddlers. They are part of the lifeblood of the centre, leading and sharing in the daily worship, taking part in the Christmas festivities and the summer outings and supporting an often overstretched staff.

New Community

But perhaps the hope of the Centre is seen best in the people who use its facilities and services. Many of the elderly people in the daycare had previously been isolated, housebound by disability, often far from family members. For them, the days had often seemed long and weary. Now they are collected from their homes by specially equipped minibuses, arriving in the centre in time for mid-morning tea and toast. They enjoy a three-course lunch, and afternoon tea and biscuits before being taken home in the late afternoon. In between they enjoy a schedule of activities which ranges from armchair aerobics to musical soirées, with quizzes, games, reminiscences, guest speakers and performers to time just for conversation. New friendships have been made, and old ones revived. Sometimes very old ones ... the delight of two ladies in their late eighties sitting beside each other and discovering they had been in the same primary one class as five-year olds was a sight to behold!

In this atmosphere, the individuality of people once again finds a chance to blossom, and you discover that Duncan and Renée are the singers in the group, that Barbara is a poet with a verse for every occasion, that there are storytellers and listeners and humorists among them — and that these people have an oral history which is a deep well to draw on. There are stories of the young girls who worked sorting the coal at the pitheads, when there *was* a coal industry; of the men who worked in the heat of the smelters, when there *was* a steel industry; stories of work and unemployment, of war and Depression, of heartache and tragedy — and yet also of courage and gaiety and faith throughout it all. Some of the deepest sharing has come in the part of the worship which is for telling stories on the theme or reading for the day. One particularly moving instance was when the reading of the story of the birth of a baby to Abraham and Sarah when they thought they would never have a child released a flood of stories from very old ladies about long-desired babies, lost children and the miracle of birth.

And the presence of children and young people in the Centre helps to break down barriers between generations. A Christmas party in the daycare is enlivened by the presence of the pre-school care bears, and together old and young play 'Pass the Parcel'. Ninety-year olds and their teenage helpers learn to see each other as individuals, not just as stereotypes to be wary of.

And the effects are not just felt within the Centre. Staff help out with problems at home, or with health, or getting in touch with relatives. All this builds confidence. One woman, talking about her mother, said, 'She never used to go anywhere. She never saw anyone. But since she's been going to the daycare, she's completely changed. You can't keep her in now, she's always gadding about somewhere!'

And around these services continue all the other activities of church and community; the craft group and the Bible studies, the dance classes and the money and benefits advice; the parents and toddlers group and the exercise classes — and the Sunday worship, for this is still a church, the Centre of a worshipping community. The Neighbourhood Centre has a mission statement:

Orbiston Neighbourhood Centre aims to encourage and develop a sense of community for all as a practical expression of and witness to Christ's love.

From the beginning, the Theology Group had wanted the Centre to be a strong Christian influence on the local community. They did not wish to go ramming the Christian message down anyone's throat, but they hoped that through their actions people would be challenged by the challenges of Jesus. That people *have* been challenged is perhaps because first of all the Group were open to the challenges of Jesus, and took them on themselves.

The End of the Book

This is usually the point where the reader comes to the end of the story. But this story doesn't have an ending because it's still happening, still unfolding, and the future is unknown, waiting to be discovered in faith. So it's the end of the book.

There are many stories like it in Scotland, more than you'd realize. One Neighbourhood Centre among many, and a small venture of faith in a sea of need. It's not unique. But it was unique to the people who ventured out on this particular sea, and interesting enough to others for many to want to know more about it. And some things about it are worth emphasizing again:

- that a group of a dozen people with no professional expertise and no particular qualifications or influence took their own experience of suffering and struggle, and allowed it to be transformed into a creative response for others

- that the churches they belonged to gave them their trust, their support and their encouragement, and in so doing, lived up to their different but linked historical callings: the one to extend the church out into the community; the other to take risks of faith and act selflessly for the sake of the gospel

- that in the course of four years, they generated £750,000 pounds of revenue and capital funding, and turned a mostly empty building into a well-equipped and staffed resource for their community, creating thirteen new jobs in the process

- that there are around fifty frail elderly people whose lives have had their quality improved dramatically, some children who have somewhere to go after school, and that there is a place where anyone can go and find welcome, non-judgemental and non-coercive acceptance, and the kind of information that could make a difference to their lives

- that in an area blighted by sectarianism, Catholics and Protestants work, pray and relax together in a spirit of openness and friendship

- that the whole project has been envisioned, planned, shaped and managed by local people, and that they have informed the local community and sought their consent every step of the way, that it is genuinely an initiative from the bottom up

- that the doing of it brought confidence and a sense of empowerment to people living in a situation of marginalization

- that they had the humility to learn a methodology

from some of the poorest and most oppressed people in the Third World, and that they maintained a global vision in the midst of a local response

- that they were accompanied by prayer, fellowship and the Bible at every step on the way, and that in that obedience, they experienced the liberating power of God

- that they found their own answer to the question, 'who is my neighbour?' They did not pass by. They were kind.

God bless them!

Appendix

Worship

Every day at 1. 30 p.m. there are prayers in the Orbiston Neighbourhood Centre. The people who had the idea for a neighbourhood centre, and who worked to make that dream come true, were motivated by their Christian faith. They wanted to share the love and care which they found in Jesus with the wider community in Bellshill. They wanted to do this in a practical way, which would involve welcome, service, and making a place where people could share not only their worries and responsibilities, but also their hopes and dreams in life, to make the centre both a safe place and a place of encouragement. They wanted to say, 'here, people are valued, people matter.'

In our daily prayers, we remind ourselves of that vision. It reminds us why we are here, and what we are about. We gather to touch the rock on which we are built.

The prayers are a time (not usually more than thirty minutes, sometimes less) where we can join together from different parts of the Centre, sing and pray and talk together, be quiet together in the presence of God. It is a time for everyone, no matter whether they are Catholic, Protestant or belong to no church. All are welcome.

The prayers are organized on a monthly pattern. Each day of the month, there is a different theme. These are things that matter to people in this community, and have been suggested by them. They include subjects like unemployment, disability, bereavement, homelessness. They also include concern for young people, elderly people, families. And there are days for new ventures, friendship, co-operation and trust-building, the necessities of life, justice. The prayers are led by volunteers, staff members or centre-users. They are simple and straightforward.

Each day, the prayers include:

- verses from the Psalms, songs of love and anger, of suffering and hope, of exile and homecoming

- readings from the Bible about the life of Jesus, and about his followers

- a time of sharing our stories, our concerns, our experience, and where we believe we see God at work in our lives, in the community and in the wider world

- prayers for the work of the Centre, for the neighbourhood, and for people or situations we are especially concerned about

- prayers or songs to express our gratitude for all the things that bring us joy and hope in life

Urban Theology Group Members

Karen Barbour

Jim Battison

Shirley Battison

John Bowman

Anita Henery

Martin Johnstone

Susan Johnstone

Evelyn Nixon

Agnes Pender

Annabelle Stewart

Robert Stewart

Nancy Thompson

The Iona Community

The Iona Community is an ecumenical Christian community, founded in 1938 by the late Lord MacLeod of Fuinary (the Revd George MacLeod DD) and committed to seeking new ways of living the Gospel in today's world. Gathered around the rebuilding of the ancient monastic buildings of Iona Abbey, but with its original inspiration in the poorest areas of Glasgow during the Depression, the Community has sought ever since the 'rebuilding of the common life', bringing together work and worship, prayer and politics, the sacred and the secular in ways that reflect its strongly incarnational theology.

The Community today is a movement of some 200 Members, over 1,400 Associate Members and about 1,600 Friends. The Members — women and men from many backgrounds and denominations, most in Britain, but some overseas — are committed to a rule of daily prayer and Bible reading, sharing and accounting for their use of time and money, regular meeting and action for justice and peace.

The Iona Community maintains three centres on Iona and Mull: Iona Abbey and the MacLeod Centre on Iona, and Camas Adventure Camp on the Ross of Mull. Its base is in Community House, Glasgow, where it also supports work with young people, the Wild Goose Resource and Worship Groups, a bimonthly magazine (*Coracle*) and a publishing house (Wild Goose Publications).

For further information on the Iona Community please contact:

The Iona Community
Pearce Institute,
840 Govan Road
Glasgow G51 3UU
T. 0141 445 4561; **F.** 0141 445 4295
e-mail: ionacomm@gla.iona.org.uk

Other Titles from Wild Goose Publications

SONGBOOKS with full music (titles marked * have companion cassettes)
SEVEN SONGS OF MARY*, John Bell
SEVEN PSALMS OF DAVID*, John Bell
SEVEN PSALMS OF DAVID - PACK OF OCTAVOS* John Bell
LOVE AND ANGER*, John Bell and Graham Maule
WHEN GRIEF IS RAW, John Bell and Graham Maule
THE LAST JOURNEY - PACK OF 15 OCTAVOS* John Bell
THE LAST JOURNEY reflections*, John Bell
THE COURAGE TO SAY NO: 23 SONGS FOR EASTER & LENT*J Bell & G Maule
GOD NEVER SLEEPS – PACK OF 12 OCTAVOS* John Bell
COME ALL YOU PEOPLE, Shorter Songs for Worship* John Bell
PSALMS OF PATIENCE, PROTEST AND PRAISE* John Bell
HEAVEN SHALL NOT WAIT (Wild Goose Songs Vol.1)* J Bell & Graham Maule
ENEMY OF APATHY (Wild Goose Songs Vol.2) J Bell & Graham Maule
LOVE FROM BELOW (Wild Goose Songs Vol.3)* John Bell & Graham Maule
INNKEEPERS & LIGHT SLEEPERS* (for Christmas) John Bell
MANY & GREAT (Songs of the World Church Vol.1)* John Bell (ed./arr.)
SENT BY THE LORD (Songs of the World Church Vol.2)* John Bell (ed./arr.)
FREEDOM IS COMING* Anders Nyberg (ed.)
PRAISING A MYSTERY, Brian Wren
BRING MANY NAMES, Brian Wren

CASSETTES & CDs (titles marked † have companion songbooks)
Cassette, SEVEN SONGS OF MARY/SEVEN PSALMS OF DAVID, † John Bell (guest conductor)
CD, SEVEN SONGS OF MARY/SEVEN PSALMS OF DAVID, † John Bell (guest conductor)
Cassette, LOVE AND ANGER, † Wild Goose Worship Group
CD, THE LAST JOURNEY, † John Bell (guest conductor)
Cassette, THE LAST JOURNEY, † John Bell (guest conductor)
Cassette, IONA ABBEY, WORSHIP FROM EASTER WEEK (ed/arr Steve Butler)
Cassette, THE COURAGE TO SAY NO † Wild Goose Worship Group
Cassette, GOD NEVER SLEEPS † John Bell (guest conductor)
CD, GOD NEVER SLEEPS † John Bell (guest conductor)
Cassette, COME ALL YOU PEOPLE † Wild Goose Worship Group
CD, PSALMS OF PATIENCE, PROTEST AND PRAISE † Wild Goose Worship Group
Cassette, PSALMS OF PATIENCE, PROTEST AND PRAISE † WGWG
Cassette, HEAVEN SHALL NOT WAIT † Wild Goose Worship Group
Cassette, LOVE FROM BELOW † Wild Goose Worship Group
Cassette, INNKEEPERS & LIGHT SLEEPERS † (for Christmas) WGWG

Cassette, SENT BY THE LORD † Wild Goose Worship Group
Cassette, FREEDOM IS COMING † Fjedur
Cassette, TOUCHING PLACE, A, Wild Goose Worship Group
Cassette, CLOTH FOR THE CRADLE, Wild Goose Worship Group

DRAMA BOOKS
EH JESUS...YES PETER No. 1, John Bell and Graham Maule
EH JESUS...YES PETER No. 2, John Bell and Graham Maule
EH JESUS...YES PETER No. 3, John Bell and Graham Maule

PRAYER/WORSHIP BOOKS
MEDITATIONS FROM THE IONA COMMUNITY, Ian Reid
CLOTH FOR THE CRADLE, Worship Resources and Readings for Advent, Christmas
and Epiphany, Wild Goose Worship Group
THE PILGRIMS' MANUAL, Christopher Irvine
THE PATTERN OF OUR DAYS, Kathy Galloway (ed.)
PRAYERS AND IDEAS FOR HEALING SERVICES, Ian Cowie
HE WAS IN THE WORLD: Meditations for Public Worship, John Bell
EACH DAY AND EACH NIGHT: Prayers from Iona in the Celtic Tradition, Philip
Newell
IONA COMMUNITY WORSHIP BOOK,
THE WHOLE EARTH SHALL CRY GLORY, George MacLeod

OTHER BOOKS
CHASING THE WILD GOOSE: The Story of the Iona Community, Ron Ferguson
DREAMING OF EDEN: Reflections on Christianity and Sexuality, Kathy Galloway (ed.)
THE PROSPECT OF HEAVEN: Musings of an Enquiring Believer, Frederick Levison
THE OWL AND THE STEREO, David Osborne
COLUMBA: Pilgrim and Penitent, Ian Bradley
THE EARTH UNDER THREAT: A Christian Perspective, Ghillean Prance
THE MYTH OF PROGRESS, Yvonne Burgess
WHAT IS THE IONA COMMUNITY?
PUSHING THE BOAT OUT: New Poetry, Kathy Galloway (ed.)
EXILE IN ISRAEL: A Personal Journey with the Palestinians, Runa Mackay
FALLEN TO MEDIOCRITY: CALLED TO EXCELLENCE, Erik Cramb
REINVENTING THEOLOGY AS THE PEOPLE'S WORK, Ian Fraser

WILD GOOSE ISSUES/REFLECTIONS
COMPASSION IN THE MARKETPLACE, Joy Mead
CELEBRATING SAINTS: Augustine, Columba, Ninian, Ian Fraser
A FAREWELL TO THE ARMS TRADE, Bernadette Meaden
A VERY BRITISH MONSTER: A Challenge to UK Immigration Policy, Stanley Hope
SURPLUS BAGGAGE: The Apostles' Creed, Ralph Smith
THE APOSTLES' CREED: A Month of Meditations, David Levison
WOMEN TOGETHER, Ena Wyatt & Rowsan Malik